GOD,
CREATION,
and
TOOLS for LIFE

ৡ Also by Sylvia Browne ৡ

BOOKS

Adventures of a Psychic (with Antoinette May)
Astrology Through a Psychic's Eyes (available November 2000)
Conversations with the Other Side (available January 2001)
Life on the Other Side (available July 2000)
Meditations (available January 2001)
The Nature of Good and Evil (available March 2001)
The Other Side and Back (with Lindsay Harrison)
Soul's Perfection (available November 2000)
and . . .
My Life with Sylvia Browne (by Sylvia's son, Chris Dufresne)

AUDIOS

Angels and Spirit Guides
Healing the Body, Mind, and Soul
Making Contact with the Other Side
The Other Side of Life
Sylvia Browne's Tools for Life

ৡ ৡ ৡ ৡ ৡ ৡ

GOD,
CREATION,
and
TOOLS for LIFE

Sylvia Browne

HAY HOUSE

Hay House, Inc.
Carlsbad, California • Sydney, Australia

Published and distributed in the United States by:
Hay House, Inc., P.O. Box 5100, Carlsbad, CA 92018-5100
(800) 654-5126 • (800) 650-5115 (fax)

Editorial: Larry Beck, Jill Kramer, Christine Watsky   *Design:* Jenny Richards

ISBN 0-7394-1005-9

Printed in the United States of America

For my beloved creators

SYLVIA'S PRAYER

Dear God,

Let this new spirit of enlightenment rinse out all guilt and fear. We come to you, God, knowing that You know not only our names, but our hearts, minds, and souls. We want to learn our lessons so that we can make the journey of life easier. We want to perfect faster than we have throughout all our lives.

From this moment on, we will love ourselves and others and let Your supreme love light the lamp of our souls. We will be imbued with love, judgment, and the will to get us on track and keep us on our perfection scheme.

We will truly be a light in a lonely desert that enlightens many.

CONTENTS

Acknowledgments ix

Introduction xi

PART I: GOD

Chapter 1:   The Nature of God...3
Chapter 2:   Father and Mother God 25
Chapter 3:   Feminine Repression 41
Chapter 4:   Our Relationship to God 45
Chapter 5:   Stories 53

PART II: ....CREATION

Chapter 6:   The Nature of Creation 61
Chapter 7:   Seven Schematics 67
Chapter 8:   Twelve Levels of the Soul 79
Chapter 9:   Soulmates 107
Chapter 10:   Physical Universe 115
Chapter 11:   Metaphysical Universe 141

PART III: TOOLS FOR LIFE

Chapter 12:   Transforming Negative Energy 179
Chapter 13:   Lights and Colors 187
Chapter 14:   Protection Against Psychic Attack....................199
Chapter 15:   Theory of Mind 217

The Tenets of Novus Spiritus 225

About the Author 229

Acknowledgments

This project is the result of many people working very hard to make my dream come true. This text was carefully revealed for you during many thousands of hours of research. I give my thanks to two people, Larry Beck and Mary Simonds, for their hard work and dedication to my mission in life.

Introduction

The Society of Novus Spiritus is my church, located in Campbell, California. The tenets in this book, the first in the *Journey of the Soul* series, are based on the philosophy of this church, which I founded several years ago. The knowledge contained in this book represents the integration of several sources of information. First, it reflects knowledge infused by my own psychic ability throughout many years. It also reflects my spirit guide Francine's tremendous knowledge of life's plan and of the Other Side. Additional knowledge was passed down from my psychic grandmother, Ada, which represents almost 300 years of psychic oral tradition. In addition, thousands of hypnotic regressions were done independently of the other material, yet it all came together like clockwork, validating it, filling in any gaps, and showing that there is a logical plan to everything God creates.

I think we as human beings have lived long enough with the so-called mysteries. As Francine says, if you can think of the question, your guides will give you the answer. Indeed, my faith, Gnostic Christianity, teaches that we must always continue to seek for our answers, because seeking is an essential process for spiritual growth.

I decided to make this philosophy public because of the reaction I receive so often: "I have always known this. This is what I have always believed, although I couldn't put it into words. I just felt that this was a truth that resonated in my soul as *right*." The philosophy, although extensive, comes without fear or condemnation. It comes with knowledge, but without dogma. I have always believed that everyone, no matter what their beliefs, should take with them what they need or want, and leave the rest. Only occultism is hidden, secretive, and controlling; you will find none of that in these writings. Of course, certain codes for behavior are innate laws of good by which we must all live—but the part of you that is God is individual in every way.

This book is organized in three parts; the first, "God," shares Francine's unique knowledge regarding Mother and Father God. The second, "Creation," articulates the divine plan and organization of the universe and our spiritual evolution. The final part, "Tools for Life," discusses ways to remain strong in the face of life's harsh lessons.

The work in *Journey of the Soul* has three voices. Of course my own is present, but I also have two communicating spirit guides, Francine and Raheim, who are the major contributors. Francine's voice is audible to me, but relaying her information orally is not the most efficient form of communication. By special arrangement with God, I am able to allow Francine and Raheim to take control of my body so that they can communicate directly with others. This is called "deep trance mediumship," which is best known through the works of Edgar Cayce. An interesting aspect of this ability is that I retain no personal knowledge of the words or actions that occur while I am in trance. For many years we have done "research trances," giving us the knowledge that fills these pages. Of course, we all learn by asking questions, so you will see many such inquiries appearing in italics throughout this work. This series is truly a journey of the soul, and I am so glad to have you along for the ride.

This material represents hundreds of hours of work, so when you read it, by no means feel that you are merely reading the faint musings of a simple medium in trance. Much of the knowledge that has been garnered is extremely deep, abstract, and esoteric; you will probably prefer to read much of it in short passages instead of all at once. I hope you enjoy it, and more important, I wish that if nothing else, you come away as I have, with a magnificent obsession to learn more, explore more, and delve deeper into the great theology that is just waiting for us to discover.

We in the Society of Novus Spiritus find that there is great comfort in walking together in our belief, loving God without fear or guilt. To learn is spiritual, because knowledge destroys ignorance, prejudice, and greed.

God bless you. I do.

— Sylvia

§ § § ζ ζ ζ

EDITOR'S NOTE: *To reiterate what was mentioned in the Introduction, the following text has three voices. Of course, Sylvia speaks, but she also has two communicating spirit guides, Francine and Raheim, who are the major contributors. Whenever the voice changes in the text, it will be marked. Also, throughout the portions authored by Francine and Raheim, there are questions that appear in italics.*

§ § § ζ ζ ζ

Part I

GOD

Chapter 1

THE NATURE OF GOD

Francine: There is a spirituality that goes beyond any religious dogma, and that is the love of the perfect God. The word *Gnostic* just means that you are a seeker of truth and knowledge about God; you are not a seeker of dogma. Dogma is man-made and filled with "cannot, should not, better not; it is terrible if you do; it is awful," and so on. God has no authorship of this. There is no place for that. The only good it does is to make people continually reincarnate until they finally come upon the pure God. The truth after which you seek is that God is simple. It is so uncomplicated and beautiful—God loves you, and you love God! Everything that gets in the way of that is superfluous.

The only thing we will take back home with us is our knowledge. That is the only thing we have to garner. Through knowledge, we love. Without knowledge, no one can love. People think they love someone or something on sight, but they do not. They feel this way because their soul knows it to be so. There is a knowledge of the other soul or a feeling of simpatico.

Without knowledge there cannot be love, discernment, fulfillment, or spiritual advancement. You may say that knowledge seems to be totally intellectual. No! It is also emotional. Along with knowledge, along the way, a burning love and desire appears. What is that called?

Emotion! Emotion begins to drive you on. That is the very beating heart of where Gnosticism or *Gnosis* ("sacred truth") resides.

It does not matter whether Jesus is the Son of God, because you all are. You all are the sons and daughters of God—no greater, no less—aspiring perhaps for a different level of spiritual growth, but that is all. Only *you* aspire to it; God does not demand it. God's love is omnipotently there. Some people are not ready to expand their mind to God's greatness and all-forgiveness; instead, they like to live with horror and the fear of a condemning God. Why that gives them comfort is beyond anything that we on the Other Side know. It seems to be a failing of human beings who are not spiritually advanced: They need to be afraid.

True Gnostics are not afraid, because they know that they stand before God with all their beauty and their soul, and they know that God is nothing but love and knowledge. God cannot have any aggravation, nit-picking, or critical judgment. If there is, if it is introduced even once, then the God we know and love is lost. But your God is the true God, which is why in the Bible He says, "Do not have false gods before me."

True religion should be exquisite. True religion and spirituality should be beautiful, blessed, loving, and filled with all goodness and love. Once you touch the hem of this, you will never go backwards! Nothing will ever be so good. Nothing will ever take the place of what you know to be the Truth. No one will ever sway you from the path of what God truly is and the blessings that He has brought upon you. You see how blessed you are in coming upon this knowledge? In coming upon it, you make God's love run freer because you are not clogged by ignorance. You have put no rocks in the path of the Love that flows toward you, and that is what ignorance does—it puts rocks in the stream. God's love is continually flowing. People put rocks in the channel so that it does not run free.

You can speak to God and be with Him anytime you choose. There are no particular hours of the day or night when God is too tired for you to approach Him. He is at your beck and call, because He not only resides in you, but outside you. Be free of what you call sin and guilt, and totally neutralized in your own beauty.

He does not care about big cathedrals. Who said that God the Father could just reside in a church? Doesn't that sound silly to you? He is out on the street. He is everywhere. He is in this room, in the lamp, in the pipes. He is much more interested in places where people can go and be together and love each other than any big golden altar. That money should be broken down and used for the poor, the homeless street people.

There is a lingering homesickness in each person for what Father and Mother God have prepared for us on the Other Side. But while you are here, you must suffer those homesick pangs. You must go through this life. You must learn, and you must enjoy it and do it without fear, guilt, or occultism.

If there is a loving God, then He made nothing evil. Life makes evil; God does not. Never let anyone tell you that you are diminished by another. All men and women are equal in the eyes of God.

I am going to talk to you in great, extensive quantity about God. First, let us start out with the question of who or what God is. In theological studies, humans with finite minds have tried to plumb the depths of their souls to figure this out. Every religion has addressed it—every possible concept has been developed—but it is still a mystery on your plane. We have also, at certain periods of your history, noted that you thought God was dead! This is only humankind's fragile way of trying to interpret something that they feel is larger than their comprehension. What they have missed is the simplicity of what God is, always was, and continues to be!

Mother and Father God

There have always been both a Mother and a Father God, so it is very hard to talk about one without the other. Now when I say to you that they always existed, it is a very difficult concept. In other words, *no beginning* is always more difficult than *no end*. This is because in your finite lifetimes, you have beginnings, but you do not want to think that there is an end. And of course there is not.

Mother and Father God always were, and that is where we get

into the problem of wondering, "When did it all begin?" Did it begin with a "big bang" or simply at some incipient moment in time? No! Everything within this life or on the Other Side, which you sometimes call Heaven, makes circles. Everything is *infinite,* which means "without end or without any sharp edges to it." I think you should know that the magnitude of Creation is far beyond most finite minds' wildest dreams or concepts.

Let us start by keeping in mind that both always were. God the Father, known as the Prima Mobilae or the Unmoved Mover, is the Uncreated Force that has always been with us. As the male persona, He is pure intellect. He has been known, at given times, to take a form, but cannot hold it for any length of time because of the magnificence of His force.

You have been taught that there is a God, and of course there is— eternal, omnipresent, and a real entity. It is not just a force or feeling; it is not nebulous. Father God cannot and will not interfere in your life, yet His love is constant and all-encompassing. He is constantly channeling knowledge about His magnificent and meticulous nature, wonderful sense of humor, and splendid creative genius. It is almost as if God took a very broad canvas, and began to paint all the things He would love. And when He painted them, so they were, and they came into being. The majesty of God is truly wondrous!

This entity, Father God, pervades all of life and holds it steady. All of life is held by His thought processes. By being held in the mind and hands of God, as it were, our continuation and our "alwaysness" is assured.

In the "beginning" of you, if you want to think of it that way, you first existed in the mind of God. Every single eternal soul—uniquely different, characteristically sound, perfect in every detail of what each was to become and evolve to—existed in this thought process, each knowing that they were unique.

You are in life for a very short, transient period of time in order to perfect and do whatever mission God sent you on, which you agreed to; you contracted for it in order to evolve and also to give data back to God for His experiencing. Also, it was decided that you would have a "life theme" and would go out and perfect your soul.

You notice that earlier, I said "for His experiencing," not for Hers—She is elevated to the point of total experience.

God in His knowingness does not have the *experience* of His knowledge, so He had to have messengers through which He could experience. And each one of you carries divine genetics! Those divine genes experience all that you experience and "fax" back all your information. God is gaining information by experiencing through your cells. So if you do not think you are part of God, think again! In the deepest form of definition, you are God, and you are part of God. Even though it might be a small part, that part unto itself is perfect! That perfectness, regardless of the overlays of behavior, keeps on perfecting.

Are you saying that we on this planet are Divine in essence?

You are a pure energy force made by God, sent by God; within you is imbued all aspects of Mother and Father God. As it has been said, you are made in the image and likeness of God. Some of you are made in the image and likeness of Mother God, whom we call Azna, and the rest of you are of the Father, who is Om.

Om splintered His creations into many divinities, which are all of us. You are a divinity! Of course, you must know that, do you not? I hope that you know you are a shard of the divine, a part of God. I hope you know that you are God. Conglomerately, you make up the feminine side of Om. In His aloneness and unselfishness, He created all of these splinterings or shards of Creation—the other part of Him—to experience.

That is the sum total of what we know God to be—pure intelligence combined with our experiences. To gain total knowledge, He must experience, because knowledge without experience is incomplete.

All these myriad souls emanated from the Divine Sparkler. These little sparks, which are you and I, very quickly began to realize that we were programmed to go out and experience. The only way to do this was to come down into bodies and lives. In a perfect environment, such as here where I live on the Other Side, you cannot experience any hardship, because my side is perfect. Even though we are evolving for God toward a point of perfection, we have none of the nuances of what your life contains on Earth, or any other planet for that matter. Most other planets do not have anything compared to what this planet holds.

Psalms 23:4 mentions walking "through the valley of the shadow of death." Here, *death* actually refers to this life. The minute you descend out of the light of the Other Side, you descend into the valley of death. It is awful to come down and have to learn. It is very much like your Bible's book of Genesis, which is probably the most valid book in the Bible, aside from some parts of the New Testament. Once you want to gain knowledge, you must be thrown out of the Other Side to come down and experience. You see, all that is factual. Everybody read it as metaphorical, allegorical, and symbolic. Yet it was actually true! The minute you need knowledge, you must now come down here.

Can you explain more about how Father God experiences? Is there anything on this planet that He does not experience?

Father God, in His equality and magnanimity, knows the end result. *How* it is experienced, even though it is known at the very end, is still data that is acquired. For example, if two people both have a life theme of Tolerance, each will experience it entirely differently. Everyone's frame of reference is different, just as with childbirth, death, or tooth extraction. You yourself made the contract that during all your lifetimes, you would also experience and perfect your theme as best you could. You, with the help of God and certain entities on the Other Side, made the choice to come down.

Not everyone can be a nun, minister, social worker, teacher, or nurse. But in your own way, you are perfecting for God. If everyone was the same, there would be no multiple levels of experiencing. Every tiny bit of experience, every tiny thought that you have, every decision you make, is part of God the Father. All of it is knowledge that He acquires. In the same way that your children have your genes, God's genes are within you.

Even the way a plant grows is God experiencing. God is learning from every single part of how you fix your house, how you drive your car, what you wear, how you decorate, and all such trivia. All of that is data. Every part of the natural world—from ants making anthills to Einstein developing his theories—forms a giant data stream. Everything that is experienced makes up the fabric of God, the conglomerate God. So you see, we can never talk about God as totally singular for any length of time without incorporating ourselves.

God the Father is patriarchal and male. He is pure maleness, not only in disposition but patriarchal rule. Please do not get the idea that in patriarchal rule there is no feeling. You must realize that the knowledge you send back has feeling, emotion, pain, hurt, and all the other millions of derivative faces of emotion. But remember this! When this emotion is fed back, it still forms pure knowledge with just the tail of experiencing.

Mother God, on the other hand, was always the counterpart, the emotional part. Now do not think that Father God's intellect does not include emotion; it is merely diminished. Similarly, in Azna, emotion is stronger and intellect is diminished. So you see, Father God has both male and female aspects within Himself, and Mother God also has both aspects. They are the archetypal figures of the feminine and masculine principles.

She, being more pure emotion, is called the Great Interceptor. When all of this Creation was started, She not only had a hand, but was the Mother of all of it. In fact, She is more of a Primary Motivator than He, only because emotion can motivate more than intellect can. Intellect is nothing but a storehouse, more like a library.

Can we go to God and protest something?

We do not get into arguments with God, but we do have arbitration sessions. God is intellect and all-knowing, so for our own knowledge, we can get into an "argument" session with God. He is totally unbiased, not argumentative. That does not mean that the part of God that is within you cannot argue back to Him. Have you not ever had an argument with yourself, with each side of the brain saying a different thing?

You see, we are all God. The part of you that is God could argue with yourself, trying to establish intellect versus emotion or the opposite. Ultimately, God, which is us, always wins, of course. The "I Am," or the true ego, argues with the "I Am"—again, for knowledge. How many times have we argued with ourselves and put ourselves through all kinds of horrors only to find out that ultimately, regardless of what pain we went through, we learned. That is what the true Gnostic finds out.

Is Mother God complete in Her knowledge?

She is complete, but She is in the process of learning through us, just as He is. But that has already been completed. God is complete with us. He needs us as the emotional side of Himself, which makes Him complete. Emotion has to have imperfections, perfections, darkness, lightness—everything for total knowledge.

Is Father God complete in His emotion?

No. He knows emotion, but He cannot perform it. Think of Him as static, as a rock of strength. Think of Her as moving through this rock—cutting through to create cities, lands, people. You might say that She is pulling from His mind the embryos of His thoughts and putting them into being. Of course, She has intellect. He has intellect, but He cannot move. We are the emotional part of His brain, the other side of it. The main source of what we are attached to is Him, because we are the feminine side of Him.

God is perfect, but do we, as His emotion, complete the mix?

Absolutely. So we are truly a triumvirate. We are the emotion of God. She is the Mover, pure emotion with intellect. He is the Unmoved Mover. Each has emotion and intellect, though. He has none contained within Himself, but She does.

Earlier, you mentioned that we were always in God's mind, and then we each came forth as individual personae. Are you now saying that Mother God was an active participant in that?

Yes. It was more like a merging than any kind of mating or copulation. They dually gave birth to Creation. The combination of Om and Azna created all that you know. The best of what they thought and wished for and wanted was made flesh. They are co-equal; they co-exist in different planes. Her dominion is physical life.

Mother God instilled in you emotion, but He, as it were, created you. You see, there are couplings all over the place. For instance, both Azna and Om have male and female aspects—and so do each of you, in your genes. So in their coupling or merging—and all of you can merge in this way on the Other Side—a birth of sorts was given to all entities. Her genes and His, still with the same identical purpose, feed data back to the Divine. Now data is not necessarily fed back to Her, although She can merge with Him at any time and receive this data. It is not as important to emotion as it is to intellect.

So She is the feeling, sensing Mother. She works out of the heart, you might say. She listens to petitions. She will intercept and move things around, where He does not necessarily have the desire or the same ability. Why should He, if the part of Himself that is Her is there to activate?

In a smaller degree, on Earth, men and women mirror Father and Mother God. Usually, men are more linear and work more out of intellect; hopefully, they also bring in emotion. Women, on the other hand, work more from emotion. Magnify that millions of times, and you can have some vague concept of how it works in pure intellect and pure emotion.

What part did Azna have in Creation?

That is a very good question. Think of the bond between parent and child—you are part and parcel of those two entities. You may not like to believe that you are part of one more than the other, but you still take on the genetic predisposition for your father's eyes, your mother's hair, whatever. In the merging of the male and female God, the genetic strain was made perfect. God had the thought in His mind, and the emotional part was actually breathed in by Azna. You could say, in a sense, that She was the "thought-birthing mother."

She was not pregnant with it, even though the ancient Gnostics believed that Sophie gave birth to humankind, but in a way, She breathed life into Itself. One had the thought, and the other gave birth. It was no different from a man wanting a child and a woman giving birth to it. She certainly would breathe Her genetic impulse in because She was all emotion. You are carrying, from the male side, the intellect or the linear thinking. She had to breathe in the emotion. It certainly is the first Creative Force.

What is the Trinity—is it the Father, Mother, and Holy Spirit?

That is right. The Holy Spirit is nothing more than the love between Father and Mother God, and between every human being— between our Gods, us, and each other. You see, when you really embrace this perspective, you begin to know that every time you face another entity, especially a spiritually good one, you are experiencing a part of the Holy Spirit. You are experiencing a part, another reflection of Mother and Father God within each and every one of you.

Pure love, or the Holy Spirit, is between Mother and Father God; the love exuded from both of them, being companionable Gods. Their love became the Holy Spirit as humankind began to incarnate, with, as Sylvia says, "your scroll in hand."

The Holy Spirit becomes so real that it descends upon you as love, directly from God to you. By calling on this energy force, it actually becomes a reality.

What does Father God do with all this data He is collecting?

What is the long-term goal? It is to constantly keep receiving data—ferociously receiving. It is gaining knowledge, for knowledge is growth and spirituality. So we might say, although it is so harsh when put into words, that God, also in His own genre, is perfecting.

Now for whom is He perfecting? The same as you are—hopefully not only for God, but for yourself, gaining wisdom and knowledge, expanding your soul.

Why do we have to perfect for God?

Because He is not all *experience*. Never enough. Experience goes on, even on the Other Side. Knowledge is constantly growing. If God got to the point that His experiencing part became static, He would not be in the process of growth, nor would we. That is why we choose to keep growing. Some stop, don't get me wrong. But most of us keep on, if we want to, perhaps by becoming guides or incarnating into life, because we want to keep learning and experiencing for God. It becomes an addiction, believe me!

If I could tell you everything that you possibly wanted to know, such as what it is like to be an astronaut, then I would sit and speak to you for hours on end. I would explain at great length about the gravitational field, and so on—but you still haven't done it, have you? Each person, being individually a spark of God, experiences entirely differently. Your self-referencing makes it all different.

It is like all of you watching an accident. Every one of you will experience that accident in a different way. Some of you will get sick to your stomach; others will self-reference back to when they almost had an accident, or have empathy for the victim, or blame the other person. A million variations of a theme! It all becomes a gigantic daily chain of reactions.

Has God had enough? There is not enough, and there will never be. That is infinity! That is eternity! If there was a cut-off, then all would end—but God cannot end. From the very beginning of time, there have been layers upon layers of experiencing. It is like saying to the scientists, "Are you ever going to be done?" No! The true scientist would say, "If I had ten lifetimes, I would still do experiments to search and investigate the universe."

Mother and Father God are melded and welded together as a dual entity. He could not activate totally on His own any more than She could. They are truly, you might say for your understanding, soul-mates. They are the other halves of each other.

Could you explain more about our life themes?

God, having all knowledge, had no experience. Knowledge without experience is not complete knowledge. So God realized, with the Goddess, that to be able to experience and know at the same time, there had to be every facet of thought that would be made incarnate and experienced. So each person then chose a theme, took it on, and began to perfect it for God. A "last lifer" takes on smatterings of all the themes. But you, conglomerately with the thought of God, decided from the very beginning that you would take themes to perfect, such as Rejection, Spirituality, Emotion, Artist, Law, and many more.

Does our past influence our current life theme?

Yes. That is why some people will say that they always wanted to be a nurse or a car mechanic, or to be able to sing or perform. It resides in a deep part of their mind. Let us say they are perfecting Tolerance—so a performer would tolerate being very much in the spotlight, as well as having to tolerate not being in the spotlight. The theme overrides everything else and perfects on its own; it is the primary motivator in our life's chart.

You can take 100 very different people who all have the same theme. Each entity will perfect differently within that theme, so every aspect and every way, shape, or form in which it can be experienced, will be experienced. The data will be fed back to the Godhead so that God in His magnanimousness will be able to know every facet of that theme. Mother God, then, is the interfering force, so if one takes on too much, She can create miracles when things have gone too far. She knows that this planet is so random. It is like having a soldier help you out of a foxhole. She arrives and gives you a morphine shot to help the pain. She is the warrior of the planet.

Why is the Mother God concept not more widely known?

Gnostics needed to hide their knowledge of Mother and Father God due to persecution by the patriarchal power structure. It was garnered by Jesus from the Essenes and the Gnostics, and was later taken by scroll to France, hidden away.

Will we ever have a true translation of the scrolls?

I do not think you need to have a "true" translation of the scrolls.

What does God think of Himself? He said "I am who am" in the Old Testament.

He would not even speak with such bad grammar.

God is truly a God of Love. Out of love, God sent people down to Earth! Some decided not to come down, and God did not condemn them, even those whose souls became dark because they separated from Him. Even those, He will not condemn. Eventually, if they do not see the Light, He will absorb them back into His mind, and they will be rinsed clean. That shows you how merciful, good, and loving God is!

Yet, too often, groups of people have been led to worship the wrong god. Even today, many worship a god of vengeance, terror, and fright. That is a false god, not our God of endless love and continuous forgiveness. The minute you give God one human trait—such as avarice, greed, or pettiness—you have created a false god. God is nothing but pure, unadulterated, unsullied, constant, eternal love. Love comes with unconditional guarantees of its continuance!

Humankind has created the idolatrous god, the one of pettiness and cruelty—but a Gnostic walks with the true God. You always hear that strange word *salvation,* whose root is *salve,* which means "a balm that is soothing" to the soul. In soothing the soul, the God of love—not of might, but of love—sustains this salve, this balm, this healing ointment. That truth has been obscured by all the supposedly knowledgeable theologians who try to make God into some kind of complex, convoluted entity. It makes us laugh.

However, the female counterpart of God does have an understanding of human qualities, only because She has had to descend to the human level and be the Ruler of the World. Still and all, in essence, She is also pure Love. But because She has to interfere in our lives, She takes on some of the human qualities. Her essence, though, includes none of the human failings. When She is no longer needed to interfere, as we say, She resumes again the anonymity of total unconditional love.

God loves you! If you know nothing else in this life, that is what you must know. Never, ever, will God turn from you. You may turn from God, but God will not turn from you. Keep that channel of loving open and pure; keep it unblocked. Too often you block it up with words, dogma, and rules. Just enjoy loving God and feeling God's love for you.

Does God feel pain? Does He ever need rest?

He does not have to take a rest; a pure energy force contains all the energy it needs. It is literally atoms, you might say, rejuvenating themselves forever—whereas the atoms in your body deteriorate.

His created forces are pure, just as you are pure energy on the Other Side. You are the genetic offspring, so you too are pure energy. On the Other Side, you do not have to go to the bathroom; you do not have to eat, although you could if you wished; and you never get tired or need to rest, although you could if you wanted to.

What if God blinked his eyes?

Here we go again. This is where people go so askew. You start putting human touches onto God. If God sneezes, does he lose 500 people? Of course not!

Does Azna appear to you a lot?

Oh, absolutely! We see Her all the time. She is always present. We are aware of Their actual beings. He cannot hold a form long. We hold our form and stay the same. They have what They *call* a form, to which we attend all the time and in which, for a short span of time, They may talk to us, love us, hold us, and be part of our lives. We get to see Her what you might call daily; then They go about Their work. But we are actually admitted to Their presence.

How do you view Father God?

I have seen Him in, I guess you might say, my eternal life span, twice. It is a light and a figure, magnificently beautiful. We actually have seen the figure of God standing. What is the feeling? I could never explain it to you.

Let me try to create a visual for you. We had a Festival of Lights a few weeks ago, which in your time was about 50 years ago. We were all centered at the big auditorium, which seats millions—now, it is hard for you to understand our space. We do not occupy the same amount of space as you do. I do not want to get into that debate about how many angels could sit on the head of a pin, but our dimensions are not the same as yours. When we say "millions," it never seems like that much.

As we were chanting, singing, and talking, all of a sudden the air got very still. We live in an atmosphere similar to your dusk light; you know how it is in your summertime right at that dusk period? That is what our lights look like all the time. Except this one time we could tell the sky started to streak, like gigantic fingers of purple and parts of red blending into orange, and we knew! Out of that gorgeous cloud mass, this figure began to appear larger than any life you could imagine! Hands outstretched, white robe, and what else can you say? It was the Face of God.

And as He appeared, He was so gigantic, and we understood why. His essence, His energy could not be contained in a small structure, except for this one and only time. Some of the elders, who had vast experience all over the Other Side or who had seen Him, said that this was the only time that they knew of in their recorded time that He actually condensed himself for a few minutes. He held the shape, though very tall, of an ordinary man. During that time, the light shot from Him and entered every one of our hearts. The eyes and the smile and the face were absolutely beautiful! A face that I could never, ever begin to describe to you and a feeling that I could never, ever be able to transmit to you. But it could not be held for very long.

The one thing that is so magnificent, which we hear all the time, is the laugh. We can hear Him laugh! We can hear His mirth! When He laughs, He rumbles and thrills and sears with such gigantic joy through our souls!

Would you describe being held by God?

Absolutely! I will tell you of my experience because we can only speak from our self-referencing. I said to our Father, "I would like to touch you." He said, "Come to me." As I did, He put His arms around me and held me close to Him, and my heart filled with such joy! It is like rejuvenation of our battery. We can do this as many times as we wish. He enfolds us in His arms, holds us, and loves us, and everything then becomes complete to us.

On the Other Side, not being the total God, we are only sparks, and we need to be rejuvenated once in a while just like everyone else. So, we surmise that He thought we all needed a shot in our hearts and our souls. So He came to us.

For Azna, however, all you have to do is touch the hem of Her garment, and She is there. She is much faster than He is. It's hard to explain; I think it's because She is a dynamic force, where He is static. He is constantly present and loving and perfectly beautiful. She is full of more fire and fury. She knows all the emotions. If you call Her, and you really seriously call Her, She is there. There is no one to whom She has not attended. She comes in many forms—some think of Her as the Blessed Mother. She will come by any form, but it is always Her. She can get rid of grief very fast. She can heal quickly. She can get rid of terrible illnesses as well as minor ones.

Azna appears young, vital, and brilliant. She can hold a form longer than Him, because emotion can, for some reason. Maybe it is because She is the original Creator, and Her strength is so magnificent! She can hold a form for a very long time. She can come in any size She wishes, perhaps dressed in Her mantle of gold, purple, and white, or perhaps in the form of "Mary" who stands atop bushes and talks to children. She gives messages out all over the world.

Our God does not seem to have a mate. From the beginning of time, He does not choose to have one that is partnered with Him. So He is the solitary God who is experiencing through all of us, whether on my side or yours. I hate to say "my side" because it is your side, too, but I reside there now and you do not. At any rate, we are the counterpart, the feminine side of Him.

When we are on the Earth plane, it is so much easier to have Her open the door, and let the love of the Mother Goddess rush in, than it is even for Father God to do so. When you once let that door open to the Mother Goddess, your whole life changes; all ancient religions had total homage to Her. It does not matter by what name She is called.

What do you feel on the Other Side?

Love! A pure energy of love! Love is the only thing that rejuvenates itself. Negativity eats itself. By hating, you could eat yourself alive, but you can love yourself well.

Earlier, you said that it was as if God painted all the things he would love, and that he holds this in His consciousness statically. Would you characterize this as an active job?

Once the artist creates the painting and hangs it up, He remembers the brushstrokes, but they are not constantly being brushed. However, it would be inaccurate to say that He created it and then put it away, completely out of His mind. It is really more that He knows it is there by His constancy, by His keeping it on the wall. He is aware of it and will not let it drop.

Azna can make the colors brighter, and She can certainly change the dimensions of the buildings or whatever might be in the picture. She can "improve" on the picture. Without seeming to be harsh, She carries with Her emotion, which, as you well know, carries with it love, vengeance, and a retributive quality. She can intercept events on your behalf.

On this planet, She is the dealer of karma. She can deal karma as She sees fit. She has been put to sleep for many years, although She was always walking through the earth. But once She has been awakened—as She always was by the Gnostic movement—people began to bring Her more to life, so to speak, in their world. Then She had absolute power to come in.

Through all the billions of people who have come through this earth, is not some of their experience a little repetitious?

I know what you are saying, and that is a very valid question. But you see, when you were made, you were made uniquely. From the very moment you came from God, you had your particular temperament, disposition, sense of humor, and every other aspect of your personality. How you view each and every tiny particle is totally unique. You did not just acquire your likes, dislikes, and temperament because you lived many lifetimes, although that has flavored you. God, in His magnificent wisdom, wanted to know every tiny nuance, even as slight as the shading of the painting may be. Even the differences between off-white, gray, and lighter gray always give off different beams of light.

Can we gain power by being together?

Yes, that is why Sylvia is always saying that when Gnostics gather together, they add to the overall strength. That is why Jesus talked about coming together in His name. Your collective Lights make more of God than if you were alone. You have more Light! Guess what happens if you have a brighter light—guess who listens and pays attention? Azna!

Which religion has the truth?

To find out who has the truth, I can only tell you to speak to your own heart. You will find out that *you* have it. Not from any so-called religious norm or a whole book of dogma, but just from coming together and aspiring to increase your knowledge.

You see, church teaching should have given knowledge, not just blind faith. This is because the greater your understanding is of God and the Goddess, the greater your love will be. Why should that have been a mystery?

Gnostics had it in the beginning. They carried it from one generation to the other until the patriarchal rule changed the rules, because emotion was dangerous to them. The truth is that you should have no fear whether or not to go to church on Sunday, or to festivals! You have nothing that guides you except knowing that you want to gain knowledge. You want to learn, not because otherwise you will be damned to hell, but only because you ought to gather together to recharge your battery and learn! That is what the early Gnostics did.

The church leaders said, "We are not getting enough members. We have to do something." Thus, hell was created! The vengeful God was brought out more. "Scare people to death! We will get more people to come!" In many ways, this Earth is fair game for that, being filled with anxiety, fear, and superstition. They used ideas taken right from the primal fear of humankind: "It's possible that God does not love me. Maybe I am alienated from God, and I will be damned." All the money in the world would then come in to build cathedrals, higher and higher, larger and larger. People were hoping that God would pay attention to these cathedrals standing around.

Then the church hierarchy got further and further away from the people, telling them that they were stupid, that they could not know, and that the mysteries were shrouded and hidden. They forgot to learn!

Intellect and Emotion

Mother God is elevated to the point of total experience. She is the totality of emotion, and this totality contains within itself the totality of experience. Does She have to experience? No! She *is* experience. The same goes for the question of whether He had to acquire intelligence. No! He *is* intellect.

The totality of our experience is for Father God, but She intercepts it all. She has Her own line to experience intellect, which She does through the Father God. He must experience His emotionalism from us; She already contains it. In the same way that He was all intellect from the very beginning, She was all emotion. He is still experiencing, but She is experience with knowledge. She already has all the emotion intact. So now, having both sides of Herself intact, She can intercept.

But you must keep in your finite mind that all Creation was made by God. When we say "God," we do not necessarily mean plural, because both are One. Just because One has a different duty or is more interfering, One is not above the other. If you have two partners in a company, one may be delineated to do one thing, and the other may do something else. Are they both powerful? Yes!

He is the hand that holds everything stable, but He cannot move. But by His very hand, everything stays stable. She is the other hand that moves within the stable hand.

He is the one who stabilized Creation and had it in His mind. She is the one who put it into motion, as emotion always does. Intellect thinks it, but the hands and eyes that move are Azna's; emotion is the mover. She is the one who actively created. His thoughts and His intellect hold us solid. That is what holds the mass together. She, however, moves and is the Creative Force.

About Knowledge

I am convinced that, to elevate yourself to any spiritual level, you must have total knowledge.

Love is constantly given to you by all of us guides and by God. It is constant, unbending, unyielding, and forever present for you. If by any means you feel that God does not love you, that is because you have shut down. God's love is a constant outpouring—nonrestrictive, nonjudgmental, ongoing, and forever present. Any god who is vengeful, mean, hateful, or nasty is, of course, an imposter. God does not play favorites, and He does not *ever* take small children—the innocents, the babies—and slay them. That kind of god is an evil created by man, not the true God.

ò   ò   ò

"God is Love, my friends—nothing more, nothing less."
— Sylvia

"Each soul is equal to the grace of God."
— Francine

ò ò ò ò ò ò

Chapter 2

FATHER AND MOTHER GOD

Francine: Azna is coming around very strongly now. Everybody should be able to feel Her. She is very strong, so powerful. When She eventually gathers Her groups around Her, She can be really strong. The world, the Earth, has put Her to sleep for so many thousands of years, yet She has always been here. When you speak the name of the God who loves you, it becomes stronger.

All the sightings of the Blessed Mother are in actuality Azna, Mother God. It does not matter what you call Her, but it certainly was Her appearing at Lourdes, Fatima, and Guadulupe. It was the Mother Goddess. She appears in all countries. You notice that you will find Her appearing as Hispanic, African, Caucasian, or Asian. She has appeared to every race and group. When everyone starts aspiring to Her, this helps Her power. Not that She does not have power of Her own, but belief itself creates its own power.

The Mother God has always been the keeper of the living and of life. That does not mean that She does not have dominion on the Other Side as well, but She rules physical life and everything that has to do with humans and human emotion. Like His work, Hers is never done. So your intellect was given to you by the Father, your emotions by the Mother. She is the only one who interferes in life. She can intercept and make better, alleviate sorrow and make less pain. If there are any miracles to be wrought, She is the one who will do it! He cannot and will not interfere, though His love is constant, encompassing, and constantly channels knowledge.

You see, all you needed was a door for Her to get through. She has been behind doors for so long. All she wanted was a crack to get through. She really is the Prima Mobilae! Now, She has come into Her own time. That really is what the New Age is dawning on. It is the time of the intercession of the Mother Goddess.

This is why I keep reiterating, without making it mandatory, that when you come together to honor Her, you loosen Her chains one more notch. Then you see what happens? She is empowered! It then begins to spread out, and the feminine principle is empowered so that it brings about peace in the world.

And none of you men should feel bad, because the feminine principle is also in each one of you; you must awaken it. In the same way, every woman must awaken her intellect. The primary and most ancient beliefs are that the female goddess was primary, and this certainly does not diminish males. Every religion has a yin and yang. Everything has its opposite. Every man and woman has both masculine and feminine qualities. This must be.

On Earth, you are taught intellect. It is pounded into you. "Get smart, go to school, or you will not get a job. Use your head. Use your mind." Isn't that what you are told? Did you ever hear anybody say, "Use your emotions?" No! We are told to control our emotions. No one ever says that if you get emotional enough you are going to get a degree. No—it is seen as a weakness that diminishes people. But emotions can create mountains.

Let us say you are having financial problems or a lawsuit. Azna will interfere and help you with this, if you petition Her. You may say to me, "Why would I petition a Mother God for money matters?" Because She can interfere, that's why! She is the crusader against negative energy. Visualize Her standing in front of you with Her beautiful golden sword, which can literally take the brunt of any negative energy.

Do not be irritated by all the small things that happen in life, because all the small and large things that happen will be brushed away. If you truly have a sense of knowing and faith in the Mother Goddess, who is the only deity that can activate, you are going to find that She can brush things away. Constantly say to Her, "Mother, You handle this."

You can even address Azna aggressively. Say: "I want this now, Azna. Please tend to me. Help me *now*." I think anything spoken aloud carries with it more power. That is why people have always prayed aloud.

So our spark of the divine is both Father and Mother God?

Yes. When you begin to express the love of Mother God, She is able to make that spark grow. You may see somebody that is a little tiny light, where other people have large luminescent lights—you can feel it. You can sense it. Each time you accept a little bit more knowledge, each time you band together, your light grows and your soul expands. She, by touching it with Her wand, Her sword, makes it expand. So you change from a little tiny cell of God into a huge cell.

I want to talk to you extensively about the beginnings of Mother God's reentry into the whole spectrum of spiritual thought. For centuries upon centuries, at least the past 20,000 years, Mother God's worship, loving, and caring was apparent. Only in the last 2,000 years has there been a patriarchal rule. In that time of the patriarchal rule, there has been nothing but chaos—holy wars, Protestants fighting against Catholics, Muslims against Jews—because dogma, fear, and guilt have been set down, which creates chaos!

You must realize that duality exists within Creation. To have just one primary source does not make any sense. The whole idea of the male-female duality has to be considered and looked at.

She is more interfering than Father God. This planet is ruled basically by the female counterpart; the duality between intellect and emotion is duplicated over and over again. Is it important for your so-called salvation to know this? No. However, it is important for the theological stretching of your soul. Being aware enough of how Creation actually began is important for your own spiritual evolvement. In fact, 90 percent of you really do not want to come back into life. You want to finish off this time, graduate, go to the Other Side, and go about your business. I cannot blame you for that, because I never want to reincarnate on this planet again, and I never shall.

I am stretching toward this Mother God, because it is a counterpart of your emotional planet. No other planet is more emotional than Earth.

With the rising of the nurturing, matriarchal God, there arises a compassionate, mollifying, loving, caring aspect of God. If linear intelligence rules, it becomes cruel, slicing, and without any caring.

If you begin to adopt this matriarchal view, whether you believe in a Mother God or not, I promise you that, from this moment on, your lives will turn around. Begin to adopt it—and not just the intelligent aspect of it, because intelligence speaks truth. But by speaking truth you begin to have the nurturing, loving, and caring; you drop all the dogmatic, ritualistic fear. Think in your own mind of the mothering aspect—what should a mother be like? A mother interferes! She makes right! She harmonizes! She gives meals! She washes! She dries tears! She communicates and makes her home all right!

However, I wholeheartedly agree with Sylvia: I do not want this to become a totally matriarchal religion without any patriarchal aspects, because that is ridiculous. Then, you are cutting off one side of the brain. The Gnostics always brought the two sides together.

I want you to deepen your understanding of the mothering concept so that you can learn to petition Mother God to interfere in your life. The male counterpart cannot interfere. That is a static, constant, unchanging, unbending principle. But emotion—which is Mother God—can move, nurture, love, soften, and make well; it can even alter your chart. Your *chart* is the contract made with God to experience certain facets of knowledge.

This is where our self-programming can come in so strongly. Sylvia has always said, "If you were meant to have an accident, then ask Mother God to intervene so that you get a nick on your fender, not a head-on collision." You still fulfill your chart.

More than anything, God wants to be loved, instead of worshiped. When you love God, then His love, which is constant for you, flows free. That is how it was always supposed to be. You must know this in the most secret areas of your heart—to love God is the ultimate!

Many people have asked me over many years, "Is there such a thing as God being an entity?" I can tell you right now that God is an entity; it is not just some kind of nebulous mind-force that moves. Perhaps you do not feel that you could ever be worthy enough to have God visit you. If that is the case, I want you to take it to a human level. Do you think your children are worthy of having you visit them? Of course! God visits you in many forms. Now, He cannot hold what we call a physiological form for very long, because His magnificence cannot hold it. But on the Other Side, you actually do view God many times in His physiological form or in a brilliant light that moves and speaks to you. She, on the other hand, being of emotion, contains a form. She is everything the ancients said She was.

The church's answer to Mother God was the Blessed Virgin. The names She has been known by do not matter. She was known as Ashara, Theodora, Sophie, and Isis. She is omnipresent! Emotion that She is, She will not enter or interfere unless She is called on; in contrast, Father God's constancy in holding us is omnipresent. But unless She is actually called upon, She will not break your privacy or interfere.

If you want peace of mind in the long days that follow, you must get some kind of help if you need it. Because on this planet, the one thing that will make you sick and ill is your emotion. I want you to consider this: When you are in a right frame of mind and your emotions are stable, nothing sets you off. But if your frame of mind and emotions are askew, then everything sets you off. Call upon Azna. She will interfere, make concessions, and create things to happen for you, while staying within the lateral movement of your chart and still allowing you to fulfill your chart.

Charts are very specific in most areas but blank out in some places, which means that you really wanted to go into a desert—into uncharted territory. When that period comes, there is aloneness, fear, and a frightening realization. You feel that death is imminent and that loss is coming. All those horrible, depressing things! That is when She is the most effective. Rather than create emotion, She comes in and stabilizes the right emotion.

Did Jesus ever mention Mother God? Was it deleted from the Bible?

Yes to both, absolutely! When Jesus said, "Mother, behold thy son," he was speaking to the Mother God, of which the Gnostics were very familiar and in whom they believed.

If the Mother God does not rise in you, or your own emotion does not rise along with your intellect, you are going to get off-track. If you are too linear-thinking, your emotion goes begging. If you do not pay attention to it, it will turn around and just smack you. The Gnostics would have nothing to do with the Bible at all. Their texts were taken to faraway hiding places.

Can we talk about the size, shape, and extent of Father God?

It is this universe! You know that there is an end to the universe, even though telescopes cannot see it. This whole universe is in the shape of a man. Now the ancient astrologers wrote that Pisces was the feet of the Great Man, Leo was the heart, and Aries was the head. Have you seen any of those archaic drawings where a man is stand-ing with his arms in circles? That was to show the created force of this God-man. Inside, supposedly, the whole dimension of God is where we reside like cellular structure.

Now I want you to think of Him as a giant silhouette of which you occupy parts. Azna, being the Mother God, is the counterpart who goes in and out creating miracles within this giant silhouette, as it were. Now, Azna does not have an altar, so to speak. Her whole dominion is physical life. From this truth came the concepts of Mother Nature, the Blessed Mother, and the Lady of the Lotus in Buddhist thought. This is the primary female ruling entity.

She moves in and out of His silhouette?

She is a freely moving God. She is the Interferer, the Mover. He is the Unmoved Mover. He is static and constant, holding everything within His own realm, within His silhouette. She can dart in and out, and be wherever She needs to be. She is not bound by a static nature.

That is why She is the overall Earth ruler.

When called, She comes faster than Om can move. His staticness is omnipotent and does not move, although it is holding, loving, giving, and caring. Prima Mobilae means "First Mover," but He does not move! But within His silhouette and His structure, He is holding you in love and encompassing you just as a mother would a child, nurturing you within His own body.

What is meant by the Trinity?

The Father God, the Mother God, and the Holy Spirit. The Holy Spirit is the love that Mother God has for Father God. This love emanates into such a force that it actually becomes almost like a separate energy that descends upon humankind. It is the love between both of them that manifests itself. You can not only elevate yourself to it, but you can ask for it to descend upon you. That is the only part that can descend; *you* have to ascend toward the rest. She can descend, the Holy Spirit can descend, but God the Father you must ascend to.

Why has this information been suppressed?

Many groups did not want it to be let out because they were afraid that they would be called heretics or maybe ignorant. But truth will always set you free! Many religions thought that by keeping people in darkness and ignorance, they could have control. Because if a mystery is explained to you, it is no longer a mystery. Not only that, but then you do not have to elevate anyone in particular. Each person can have just as much knowledge as the next.

Religion, tragically, has held you under the thumb of what they wished you to know, thinking you were too stupid to encompass any larger aspects. That is not true, because some place in your soul will resound to the fact that you come from countless millennia.

Men, in those early days, feared the emotion and abilities of women, and they did not want any woman to know that there could be a feminine part to God, because that would empower the female!

And empowering her would give her the same spirituality as men. If it had started out that women had power, then we would have also had a matriarchal rule; then, we might not have had any wars. So what they should have done is acknowledge the duality, which of course is matriarchal and patriarchal rule. It is the same as if you just used one side of your brain. You would be all emotion or all dull intellect.

They were terribly afraid to bring in the passive, sweet, convivial, loving side, because that does not bring about a lot of money. That does not bring fear either. It certainly does not bring a lot of people into a church!

Does Azna rule just Earth, or other planets as well?

Other planets as well. But She deals with your side more than my side. She is the miracle worker. She is omnipotent, dealing in the flesh-and-blood problems of everyday life.

Why was Azna quiet for so long?

Because this whole world had to go through its own traumatic evolution. It had to go through its whole learning process. You must do it not only individually, but collectively.

And until the group came down that were proponents of Her name, She had to be, as you might say, asleep. However, She was never truly asleep. She was moving all around, but nobody paid any attention to Her. Has She always been here? Yes. Was She given acknowledgment? No.

If you give power to goodness, it grows. If you give power to negativity, it rampages. So too on this plane.

Why did She not from the very beginning make Herself known? She did in the very beginning—until the patriarchal rule began 2,000 years ago. Until that time, the Gnostics were running everywhere, trying to bring forth the truest religion of all. You see, it started out with the true religion, the duality, but that did not make any money, or build a big church. So somebody decided, "Let's make a really mean, nasty god. This will scare everybody to death."

Look at your cathedrals. Why would you need such grandeur? You might need a large place to meet, but certainly God does not need all that expense.

What does it mean to give yourself up to God?

Saying it, meaning it, and doing it must be an affirmation that is done every day. Then, slowly at first, the fears begin to fall away, even those about money and being loved. Keep repeating: "I am resting in your hands, in your heart, O Mother and Father God. Please lead me, direct me, give me peace, show me the way."

But be specific when you pray, and also add that you are able to handle any repercussions from what you have asked for. But if I were you, I would ask for peace of mind, health, and joy, but not to the point where you become placid. If you have these things, then everything else will fall into place, because humanity's total thrust is to be happy.

Believe me when I tell you this: God wants everyone to be happy! God never wanted anyone to be sad. I don't care what you have been taught or whether anyone preached that you are supposed to live a life of suffering. That is not what God has ever wanted for humankind. God wants every person to seek happiness, and every person to evolve in their own space and time—totally loved by God, not disdained by Him.

When you address God, you do not have to go through lengthy prayers, penance, or supplications; you do not have to beat your chest. Simply say, "I am here, God. I know that You are present with me. I love You, as I know You love me." That's all! God's love pours through you and gives you all the help you need.

Always remember, in your prayers, to ask specifically for what you need. Say, "Azna, I want . . ." In many ways, you will find that you are more protected now than you have ever been. That does not mean that you do not bump yourself, hurt yourself, or have things happen. People still die; things go on. But there is a lifting of the spirit, of pressure, heartache, and suffering. Even if you have to go through the things that are dealt out in this life, you will do it with much more grace and ease, because She is the activator. She creates—in fact, She is the only one who can create an intercession in your chart. This means that if your chart gets too much for you, and you have bitten off more than you can chew, She can make that uphill road flatten out.

You must ask Her for this intercession. Tell Her, "I cannot take any more. Azna, please eliminate this." This does not in any way hinder your growth. You just have a right to pull on the chain when it gets to be too much. It is sort of like giving birth—you are breathing and breathing, and your coach is saying, "Okay, if you breathe faster and relax more, then you will give birth to your new self."

The one thing that we find with you human beings in physical form is that you have always been taught not to ask for too much. It has been taught and drummed into you: "Why do you not thank God? Why do you ask for so much?" God does not care if you thank Him or not. She likes to be thanked, but She is not going to get mad if you do not. Our Gods are beatific and will not be thrown or assuaged by any of the human characteristics that you like to put on Them.

So you must ask for as much as you can, for as long as you can, and for as many things as you can think of! If you don't, you will not get them.

She is the one to be petitioned; She expects you to ask. So many people have said that after they send out their petitions, they ask for a flower to be delivered to them—and many times, they have gotten a flower within a few days from an unknown source. Somebody gave them a rose or a lily. She loves to do this because She is the miracle worker and She has the power to create such things. If you don't believe, it doesn't matter to Her.

Should our prayers be directed to Father or Mother God?

You do not have to be that definitive. If you pray, whoever is there catches it. You do not have to worry about, "Now I am praying emotionally, so I am going to pray to Her. Now I am praying intellectually, and addressing Him"—no. Now we are going into that dogmatic thing again. You have got to realize the understanding and knowledge of these beings is so massive that you do not need to be so definitive.

The only way you can truly find God is inside, not outside. People are constantly looking outside themselves and are fearful that, ultimately, God will not protect or take care of them. But if you throw yourself totally without reservation on the mercy of God, you will always be protected. However, to you, the Mother God seems to be reticent sometimes, not helping and being absent from you—you can even be mad at Her for not answering your prayers. You see, Her time and your time can be different, and She knows that. Sometimes She must stay Her hand because you have a lesson to learn. When that is learned, She steps in and answers your prayers. Now, you can be experiencing for yourself, or you might be unfortunate enough to live an exemplary life, like Sylvia, who has to be an example for so many people.

I think one thing that Azna has tried to bring in with the sweep of Her mantle is that everyone should be very, very much imbued with the self and the God-self. That is what the mantle of Azna brings: finding God within yourself, your own God-Centeredness. It bursts forth, and the soul gets so large it begins to bang on the outside. It does begin to magnify the Lord, the Goddess, everything! Once it goes inward like a lamp, it turns outward like the lotus petal. That is why the Buddhists use the lotus petal, because it springs forward in such beautiful purple hues. The seed that is planted grows—but nobody notices it until it bursts into bloom. So it is not selfish to want to have water for your own flower garden. If you do not have that, then no one can enjoy it, and you are just a little dirt patch sitting there waiting for somebody.

What kind of form does Azna take?

Beautiful. Absolutely gorgeous. She is tall, willowy, and beautifully figured, with a radiant face, alabaster skin, and large luminescent eyes. I have seen Her with both a light and dark complexion. She will be seen dark-haired. She will also appear Hispanic or black; She can change into any visage. However, the eyes seem to be always luminescent and beautiful, almost strangely oval-almond shaped.

Mother God is tall, and by your standards She might seem buxom-looking. She is very, very voluptuous. The Father, on the other hand, is very tall and stately looking, with very dark coloring and eyes. They have always taken this form for us. Beautiful-looking, the way you would think a God and Goddess should look. Father God has almond-shaped eyes; He is almost what you would call Asian-looking. She has much fuller features. There are little physical aspects that you can see in each One from which They created every race on Earth. There are parts of Their features or structures all over the painted canvas; it is quite beautiful.

Not just a chosen few are able to see Azna. Anyone could see Her, if they really, really want to. I do not just mean that you must believe, but actually ask to see Her!

Why doesn't She appear to us more?

I think it is the same principle as the burning bush. If you saw Her every day, what would you have to perfect? Sometimes the absence of the Divine helps you learn how to sustain your knowledge and keep on going. Otherwise, it would be too easy.

What every person should have is the symbolism of the God-Centeredness (or that of any messiah). Focus on not just the man Jesus, but on what it really meant to pick up the crucible like he did, trying to save the world from patriarchal rule and trying to bring Mother God into the world. Even at the very time of his crucifixion, he saw a vision of Her and said from the cross, "Son, behold thy Mother. Mother, behold thy son." Everyone wrongly thought that he was talking to his birth mother standing at the foot of the cross, when he was actually talking to the Mother Goddess. He was trying to bring about, even in his weakened state, the Mother Goddess concept. The Egyptian rule elevated women, such as Cleopatra, Hatshepsut, and Nefertiti.

Once you get it through your thick human minds, then you can serve God and get more blessings by love and acceptance of what is true and by continuing to learn, study, and seek knowledge. That is what the true "magnifying of the soul" will mean: to keep searching for knowledge. Yes! I have been searching for many years. I have only had one lifetime, and I am also a spirit guide—which will make up for a lot of lifetimes—and I have not even scratched the surface of that gigantic painting. I have not even begun to take one little fleck off. So you can imagine the magnitude of knowledge that is yet to come. It becomes, as Sylvia always says, "a magnificent obsession." Each corner that you peel back reveals another prize, and then another and another. Each one enlightens you more.

Can certain people petition God better than other people? Sometimes yes! That does not mean that anybody is less, but a person who works tirelessly for God certainly has a better voice than most people.

How spiritual are "primitive" peoples?

Many times, they are much more spiritually attuned—not necessarily more highly evolved, but they certainly can evolve more easily because they do not have the nonsense of dogma. Compared to our society, they have less mental illness and sickness, and hardly any insanity. All indigenous peoples from the African continent have this tremendous love of Mother Earth, Mother God.

Reaching Out to Others

Sylvia has always been a proponent of serving *other* people whenever there is anything wrong with you mentally, physically, or whatever. The more you practice reaching out, the better off you will be. That is an absolute fact. It is a guarantee, and I have no problem saying that from God! It is one of the universal laws that guides everyone who has ever come into life, and it still guides us on the Other Side when we come back.

One universal law is this: "As much good as you do for other people, you are then guaranteed that your life begins to stabilize. Your mental, physical, and spiritual health gets better." That is an absolute from the very beginning of time. There are not very many universal truths, but this is one! An absolute! That is directly from the mouth of God! The more you give out to, care for, and love other people, the more happy and healthy you will be.

Have you ever noticed that the people who work tirelessly for others are the ones whose health holds up, even though they may get tired. I do not mean that they do not eventually die, because that is the truest blessing of all. As I have said to you many times, death is a reward for living!

So the more devotion you have to Azna, the more clout you have, because of course that makes the bond stronger. Who is the Mother going to listen to? The one who speaks constantly to Her and is loving and caring, or someone who neglects? And more than He, She loves the pomp and ceremony—the adoration, love, and caring.

Now, December 8 is Azna's feast day. On feast days, you honor that God. In ancient times, in whatever culture and by whatever name She went—whether it was Isis, Theodora, or Ashara—people would bring flowers and burn candles on Her feast day, because that does something for both you and Her. Your petitions change many, many things in your life.

The ancient Asians had a great love of Kali, a Hindu goddess. They had great respect for the feminine side, although She was always supposed to have been the destroyer. By no means do I want to give you the impression that Azna is a destroyer. But I will tell you this: She is not somebody to make mad. I do not mean by your actions; I mean that when She feels that Her mantle of protection is around you, and you have accepted Her, then beware anyone who really hurts you after that. Her vengeance is very swift. I think that is where they got the impression that She was a destroyer.

Is our spiritual quest to become as close to Him and Her as possible?

Yes, absolutely! And that does not mean that you will ever lose your individuality. There are some who believe you will go completely back to the heart of God and be absorbed. No! You keep your individuality, but what you will do is become more magnificent, more like God. So what you are becoming, whether you want to believe this or not, is *godlike*.

You yourself, while not becoming gods, will become godlike! That is your ultimate goal. It is the same for countless other entities who emanated from the Divine Sparkler and have become godlike under the auspices of the contract between you and God. Through all the eons on which I can look back, I do not see any individuals becoming God, but many have become godlike.

Your essence—what you are made of—has continued with you through all eternity. This essence, which is part of God, was individually sparked in you, uniquely shaped and formed, and sent on its way to return in its individuality back to God. You will never lose this particular shape, the very core of your being. The reason I am making a point of this is that so many religions have claimed that when you eventually reach a level of perfection, you go into some type of nebulous form and get lost in a sea of anonymity. But the truth is that when you take on this individual essence of God, you are elevated to a point of godliness.

Most people are afraid to admit out loud that they are God, that they are part of God. You are! In doing this, you have a divinity. This has nothing to do with ego. It has to do with the divine spark of your perfection. Any behavioral overlays that you may acquire from life have nothing to do with your divine spark. Cross, cranky, infirm, ill, mean at times, not feeling good—these have nothing to do with the individual essence that you have acquired from the Divine. That has only to do with the behavior that is acquired from living life.

Seeking Knowledge

The ultimate spirituality is knowledge and more knowledge. It is pulling back from your own morphic resonance—that is, your own past-life memory—a time when many of you walked the sands, spread love, healed, and took care of the lepers. Many of you gave out love and understanding. You got rid of all prejudices about race, sexuality, and everything else. You took care of all the people torn away from their homes, who felt abandoned, who were told they were wrong, that their souls were damned to hell. You were the salve givers, adding balm to their wounds. In doing this, your spiritual soul was like God, all forgiveness. You emanated the "Godness" in the world. You then actually became a light in a dark world.

As I have said to you so many times, it has been our policy and our belief that if you do not want to do this, if you feel that it is wrong within your heart, then please go with God. Sylvia has always said, "Take what you want and leave the rest." This is the way it must be!

᭡   ᭡   ᭡

"Where are you going?" said my soul, in a quiet corner all alone.
"I'm going where I please," said my willful heart.
"I have passions to be spent, and life in abundance to live."
"I am intellect," said my head. "I can rationalize everything. I
have mind-power to learn, and mouths to listen to,
and books to read."

"Do you know where you are going?" my soul again replied.
"I am full of muscle and bone, and I must excel to live," said my
body. "But," said the soul that breathes with God, "all these are
nothing until you bring them into harmony with Me."

— Sylvia

᭡ ᭡ ᭡ ᭡ ᭡ ᭡

§ Chapter 3 §

FEMININE REPRESSION

Francine: The defeat of the feminine principle has been horrifying. I would like you to think about the Bible in this regard. The Bible debases the female from its very beginning, in hopes of denying anything that had to do with the feminine side of God. Thereby, the patriarchal side of God rose higher. That is not wrong, but the patriarchal aspect, as you well know, is intellect—stagnant and constant with no feeling.

The Book of Genesis immediately gives Eve an evil connotation by saying that she is the one who led Adam astray, which sets the tone that anything feminine is bad. The Bible is a very young book compared to most of the ancient religious texts, most of which glorified women and the feminine principle of emotion, which should also be in every man. The writers of the Bible also conveyed the notion that a woman was unclean. She was to be put out during her menstrual period. She was thought to be foul, and it began to be thought that anything feminine was lesser.

Azna has been quiet, as She is in many societies, although no society has ever buried Her like Western culture. But She began to rise up using the voice of the Gnostics to bring Her back. Really, in your era of the late 1950s when they proclaimed, "God is dead," in many ways that was true because they tried to kill Her off!

The male hierarchy wanted people to follow like sheep. This kept the patriarchy going, but in every religion there was always a feminine god, whether it was Ashara or Isis, always to exalt the feminine principle. But that is not the case in modern society! You cannot neglect a god or a principle of divinity for very long without having everything go askew.

As the feminine and masculine principles come together in your own mind, they are welded together and everything begins to be balanced. Why has man not realized that in all Creation there is a male-female duality? There must be for it to reproduce itself—in this case, to recreate the Word. So you, being the manifestation created by God who also carries the genes of Mother God, will now push Her up to Her elevated position.

During the Inquisition, who was put to death? Mainly females, because it was declared that they were witches who had intercourse with the devil. Can you imagine what kind of idiocy, what kind of mental midgets would have thought such an idiotic thing? And yet, even though you are not in the Dark Ages, you are still living in an ignorant age of darkness. People still believe that you have to go through Jesus to get to God. What did people do before Jesus was around? Did God say, "I am not going to listen to you until Jesus comes"? See, this is not a matter of faith—just common sense. You will be the ones to bring the light to people. Small and powerful as you may be, you are the ones who will carry the Word. In doing that, Azna will bless you. She knows who Her soldiers are.

Early Gnostics were not put to death for believing in Jesus. They were put to death for believing in the feminine principle! For this belief, they were thrown into the lion's den. At that time, the patriarchal church was already well established, because Rome was ruled by what? Men! The Sanhedrin, or court of the Jewish legal system, was also ruled by men. Jesus was very masculine, yet he wanted so much to bring about this soft, caring, nurturing consciousness that is the feminine principle, and no one listened!

Coming together in God's name really brings about a power that protects you! Religions have always said you must come to church because God will be angry if you do not. That is ridiculous! Nothing bad happens if you do not go to church. However, when you do, good things come to you. There is power in togetherness. That is what Our Lord tried to tell people, as did Buddha and Mohammed—but then church leaders took that and changed it. They said, "Now we will build a giant church, everyone will pay us money, and we will scare them. If they don't come, God will be mad at them, and they will go to hell." That is wrong!

You are protecting the one spark of the God-power that is different from any other spark that exists anywhere in the universe. That should make you so terribly proud! The spark of God that emanates through you is never duplicated again! It is part of God's cellular structure—part of His great creative force of which you are a genetic product. So you have the highest form of genes from Mother and Father God. You are to carry that light on! So, you see, you can never be separate from God.

Affirm the following frequently: "I am the sum total of my perfection from God. I am the sum total of my God-Centeredness. I am the sum total of the Mother Goddess." In doing that, the sum total of this beauty of your soul then begins to rise up. You are not so concerned about how warm, full, happy, or nurtured you are, or how much you need. Most of you will find that in this spiritual time, you are going to get tremendous reciprocation from the Mother Goddess. I mean that! You are going to get reciprocation.

In essence, what Azna does is to create a more optimistic environment. Now I know what you are going to say to me: "But how can I help it when I get afraid, anxious, or depressed?" You have got to realize that this is part of the challenge of going through the labyrinth of life. You must not be too cruel on yourself for that. It is terrible to worry about money, health, lousy children, burdensome parents, things that bother you, and illnesses that creep in. You cannot be happy all the time—but I think that sometimes instead of trying to fight against these things, you must go with them. In other words, you have got to say, "All right, give me your best shot. I am going to come out of this okay."

ॐ   ॐ   ॐ

"If you keep the light, your light will kiss another's.
We will find you and kiss your light!"

— Francine

"People are afraid to die, and even more afraid to live."

— Sylvia

ॐ ॐ ॐ ॐ ॐ ॐ ॐ

§ Chapter 4 §

OUR RELATIONSHIP TO GOD

Francine: God on the Other Side is like a sprinkler system. He is omnipresent and always there so that you can plug into that, yet He is a real entity. Please do not think of God as just a force. He is a force, but He and She are also actual entities. They do have and can hold a form for a while, which is a force with a persona and a real, individual personality.

It is magnificent in its entirety. What gives us such great, glowing pride is that we know we have added to the experience of this Being. It is not only complete unto itself, but we add to it, which means that we can never be separated from the Whole. We are not only part of the Whole but separate from the Whole and carrying inside of us part of the Whole. So the whole aspect, then, is complete. No part of the pie is missing. None of us can be diminished. Each one is just as magnificent as any other.

You may be overwhelmed and feel so small, as if you are an infinitesimal part of countless billions of entities—but please do not! Each hair on your head, each finger of your hand is singular. That is the way it is to God. When you come over to the Other Side, you will understand that your essence is magnificently bright and significant, although you do not know this in life. One of the things you lose in life is the significance of yourself. That is what is so hard. Your ego becomes so bruised, lost, and diminished. On my side it becomes so gorgeously inflamed, brilliant, and unique. That is why all of us spirit guides try to instill a purpose in you regarding the mission you have and the omnipotent, beautiful elegance and uniqueness that you carry—"the splendor of self," as Sylvia says.

False Worship

Sylvia: I want to talk to you about Father God. I want to talk to you about how much we have maligned, abused, falsely worshiped, and been disturbed by the current view of Father God.

"In the name of God," down through the centuries, we have done many disturbing things: We've shaved our heads, gone into monasteries, become celibate, flogged ourselves, slept on nails, and gone after the Holy Grail, which does not exist. In doing all this, we have stated that it was in the name of God.

Soon after Jesus' coming, we fought "holy" wars. Now there is an oxymoron! There is nothing holy about a war! We still have such iniquity in the world. "In the name of God," we have created more atrocities than any one person or group could ever think up. In truth, all of it has been in the name of idolatry, not God.

The Commandments say, "You shall have no other Gods before Me." I believe in that particular Commandment—some of the others can be challenged, but that one is valid. It means that you should not worship the wrong god—namely, a fearsome god. Please ask yourself, why are we worshiping a god of fear? Of vengeance? Where is the God of love, the One who lovingly put us here? Which god is *the* God?

Stop and think logically! What sadistic god, what monster, what horribly Satanic type of god would put people on Earth only to suffer in life, then end up in hellfire and damnation, to lose people we love, to be with hurt children and homeless or crippled people? Do you think it is simply a toss of the dice? Or do you think that if you're not nice, your child or spouse will be taken away from you? Is all this suffering at the whim of a petty, jealous god? I don't think so!

In rebuttal to this image, so-called psychics came along and said, "Well, the reason you are suffering now is due to your bad actions in a past life." This is not true either! However, we can bring things to this life related to other lives, such as guilt and fear and all those things. But very rarely is it ever a retributive situation.

The pains in life are tests that we picked to perfect our soul. We have a contract with God to experience His knowledge, test our soul, and become a better person for doing so. We choose to have problems in order to experience for God. God did not command, "You are going to be a victim, wallow in pain, be poor, and have sores on you." What kind of a parental figure is that?

The true God of Love allows us to go through school—that is, through the hard knocks of this life—because it makes us better people. How many times did you hear this when growing up: "Well, if you don't listen, you have to learn"? Did anybody ever say that to you? They said that to me until I was blue in the face! God said, "If you want to perfect your soul for Me, if you want to be My emotion and experience, you have free will and the choice to go into life and endure it for Me." And we said, "I love You so much because You are Love. If You need me to experience for You, I am going to go down and do a good job. I am going to learn and bring information back to You."

Then we got down into life and the world began to fill our heads full of all kinds of erroneous stuff. Not the simplistic stuff such as "God is Love," because that does not make for big business. And we bought it, didn't we! Maybe some of you did not buy it, but said, "What kind of God is that? I'm so afraid of Him! Am I supposed to love Him or fear Him?" You cannot do both! Two opposite emotions cannot reside together. You must either love or fear. Which is it?

We must choose to love God. It must be! The love of God is why I am doing all of this. I do not want to say, "Look at the pain You put me through, God!" Not at all. I did it to myself, but most people do not like that. We do not like to be responsible for our situations. We want to blame someone else, even God, for our misfortune. Yet on the Other Side, we were so happy when we did it. "God, I picked a tough one this time." Or an easy one, or some of each. "But hopefully, dear Father, I won't gripe about it every single step of the way, because when I get into human form, I get stupid and forget." We all do. We have our memory of the Other Side shut off, because if we had that memory, it would be easy. Then there is no test for the soul.

Your contract is with God: You get to elevate and perfect your soul, and He gets the information you send back. How many mothers do you think have scrubbed floors for 15 years so that they could send their children to school? How many people sacrifice every single day of their lives? That is very much like what we are doing in life. We said, "I will do anything for You God, because I am Your child. I'm part of You. You are part of me. I am God. Of course I will go on this mission for You. I will go down and be happy about it, because I will learn things. I will really be tougher than most, because most people never choose to come down. I will be good. Maybe I will go through cancer, loss, heartache, war, or fire, but I will do this because You need information. You are all knowledge, and I will be the experiencing part. I cannot know heat unless I touch a flame, nor cold unless I hold ice. I am going down to experience for both of us."

So we came down the chute merrily into life. Then we got here and said, "Oh, damn! This is awful! I may have picked this course of study, but now I don't want to do it." Tough! You picked it and must fulfill it, but you could do it with a smile, because you are really perfecting for yourself and elevating your soul to God. Sure it hurts! It's like a bad pair of shoes that you have to go walking in. It hurts for that time. But after you take off the shoes, you only *remember* how bad your feet hurt—memory is a far-off thing. That's the way it is when we get to the Other Side. It all becomes a vague memory. Ask any woman to stand up and recreate childbirth pain. They cannot. If we did, we would never have a second child. No way! The memory of pain fades. Physical pain, as well as mental pain, goes away fast.

So our loving God stands there and watches us. I can see Him saying, "They made the contract and chose to go down. They told me they would do it. Now all I hear is griping!"

Sometimes I look back on the hard times I have gone through, and it's all just a vague memory. I can look back and pretty much understand that Sylvia was suffering. But it's past; it almost seems to be another lifetime. You can do the same thing. You can stand proud and say, "But they didn't kill me. I am strong." Remember, they cannot eat you!

Have you ever met one of those people who says, "I've had a wonderful life. Everything is perfect and great." They are insane! They are nuts! That is the kind of person who talks to walls. There is not one of you out there who has not had your suffering and pain. It is all relevant to you.

People come to me for a reading and say, "I don't want to tell you this, Sylvia, because it sounds silly." I say, "No. If it's real to you, it's real to me," and it is. Who's to say that a paper cut for one person is not just as bad as a big gash for somebody else?

Now does that make us wonder how stupid we were over there? No. Sometimes we walk around saying, "What was I thinking about when I wrote this? What was the matter with me? If it's really true, Sylvia, that I wrote this, was I crazy?" No. You were at the highest point of intelligence! The tougher the stuff you picked, the more you wanted to gain in prestige, honor, and spirituality. That is what we wanted—to get the gold ring. There is nothing wrong with that kind of pride and love. There is no false ego involved when we say, "God, look at me. Aren't you proud of me?" Absolutely. The same as you are with a child. You are proud of that child. Now imagine God's love for you magnified billions and billions of times. That is the God that we worship. That is the God that we love.

Interpreting Dogma

It is interesting to see how the Dead Sea Scrolls and modern archaeology are changing our view of the Bible. For instance, the Bible tells us that the walls of Jericho came tumbling down in a battle, but in actuality there was no city of Jericho at the time of that battle. And what about the stories of Jonah in the whale, and all the animals in Noah's Ark? You should look at these stories as parables trying to show God's love. "God is so great," they were trying to say, that he could do these things. But people said, "Oh, this is literal. I have got to write this down. This is the Word of God."

The Bible was written in parable. As it says in the Dead Sea Scrolls, Jesus told the disciples that he spoke in parables to the masses. "But," he said, "those of you who know the keys will know the Truth."

For centuries, our wonderfully loving God was made into a false god of vengeance, pettiness, and humanistic qualities. If pure love and pure intelligence exist, there can be no avarice or greed; such an entity cannot play favorites, have vengeance, or make a devil. Because if God makes a devil, that means He had to have evil within. Be reasonable. You cannot make what you do not know.

So the early religions inverted the true God of Love. They made a vengeful and mean god and a devil to scare everyone into obedience. The early religions made people fear god and convinced them they were sinners. They said, "We will crucify anyone who tries to challenge our power. Then we will tell everybody he died for their sins!"

Yet some of us walked around saying, "But I didn't do that to him. I *wouldn't* have done that." But the Church said, "Yes, you would have and you did, and now you have to pay for it." To make this even more ridiculous, Jesus did not really die on the cross. I have said that for years and been called a heretic. But now, the Dead Sea Scrolls are proving me right! For one thing, figure it out yourself: A strong, healthy man of 33 years is not going to die after hanging for three hours. Even Pontius Pilate expressed surprise at this. Usually they hung for several days.

To be a true Christian, follow Jesus' teachings. We do not need to focus on his death in order to appreciate his greatness! The terrible horror he went through on the cross is not needed to validate his teachings. If you do nothing more in this world, please approach your religious and spiritual beliefs with knowledge. Do not ever approach anything with blind faith. That is one of the most awful concepts around. And never approach things with guilt.

It is so simple—God is Love! You came here to fulfill your contract, which you will do whether you like it or not. It is nicer if you do not gripe about it, but if you do, so what? All of us will face hardship and tragedy. I know I have, and so will all of you. But regardless, we are all going to graduate eventually.

Time condenses and seems to be going faster these days. Have you noticed that? Francine says that time is speeding up, because we are getting to the end of things. And please forget about the "rapture" because Jesus does not want to come down here anymore. Would you? No. Francine says that we are in the "time of the Messiah." When she first told me that, I could not understand what she meant. She said, "The Messiah is coming again, but in the form of True Thought. Jesus will be resurrected to what he really was in the beginning." That is the rapture! He is not going to appear in the sky with a sword. Why would he appear with a sword? He was the most kind, loving person in the world. He is supposed to slash the bad on the left and take the good on the right? Nonsense! What if you were born in Africa and never heard of Jesus? You cannot tell me that God hates those good, wonderful people.

I have been to Kenya many times. I would go back in the bush and see the natural beauty and spirit the people have. If those souls are not going to Heaven, then I do not want to go. If all the people of the world who do not know Jesus are damned to hell, then I do not want to go, because only an evil god could do such a thing.

In truth, all of us will go back to live with the Father and Mother God. That is the true Heaven; there is no hell. We are going back to the God that we love, who loves us unconditionally. But you might say, "I'm a sinner. I have done terrible things." So have I; so have we all.

Does love fill churches? No! Fear does. Fear builds big cathedrals! It makes people fall to their knees, bend their heads, and strike their breasts. Imagine a loving God looking at this! If your children fell to their knees in front of you and hit their chest every time they walked in the room, then what kind of a parent would you think you were? Something would be very wrong with that.

If you come from the position that God is Love, you will be all right. Just say, "God, my day is spent for You. Know always that my heart is with You, through all my faults and foibles." I know that God knows my heart. He knows where my Truth is, even with human failings. He knows that my motives are right. And so are yours!

§   §   §

"The belief itself is very simple: Do good work,
love God, and—as Sylvia says—shut up and go Home!"

— Francine

"This belief system makes God stretch.
It lets God really be God."

— Sylvia

§ § § § § §

Chapter 5

STORIES

Francine: There are a lot of people who come in and tell Sylvia great stories. This one shows a true miracle by Azna!

Azna's Bundle

A woman named Holly came in to see Sylvia and said she once had a son by the name of Aaron. He was playing by the pool, but he was locked in a playpen. She went into the house to answer the phone, but first latched the pen Aaron was in. Holly said, "As I was talking on the phone, I heard the silence."

She ran outside, and Aaron was no longer in the pen. She ran out front, searching; then she got this horrible feeling and ran back to find Aaron at the bottom of the pool. She was screaming and screaming and screaming. "At that moment," said another woman named Mary, who lived three doors down and could not possibly have heard, "something came out of the air and said to me, 'Get down the street.'"

Neither Mary nor Holly believed in spiritual matters. The next thing Holly remembered was a woman banging on her gate saying, "Let me in. I can do CPR. You go in the house and call the fire department." So Holly left the child with Mary, ran in the house, and called.

In her crazed state of mind, Holly sat in the middle of the street, afraid that she was going to miss the fire truck. As she was sitting there, she looked up. In the sky right above her appeared a throne, the most gorgeous throne she had ever seen. On this throne was sitting a woman, and in her arms was a bundle. He was all in swaddling clothes, which symbolized death. That is what Jesus was put in, swaddling clothes. Now if you covered a child up to the neck, he was alive. If you covered up the whole body, he was dead.

The woman sitting on the throne, Azna, extended this bundle to Holly and said, "You can have this back for eight years, and then he will be restored. Do you want this precious life back?" Holly said yes, recognizing somewhere in her heart that this must symbolize her child. She went back and found out that Aaron was going to live. He was in a coma for a while, and when he came out, he was very deformed.

Aaron never grew that much, but he could play and sit in her lap. Every single day of her life after that, caring for this child, a miracle happened. Some miracle somewhere. Many people came who had heard about the child; they were blessed and made well.

Eight years later to the day, Holly was in her closet, and a voice right out of the air said to her, "Your child has been restored." She looked up, and there was a little white figure running joyfully across the floor. The night before that, for some strange reason, she'd said to him, "Aaron, someday you will play and be in your big wheel; you are going to be running free."

Holly went to her husband after she saw this little white figure running across the floor. She said to her husband, "Please go check on Aaron. He is dead." He said, "Don't be silly. I was just in there." But in fact, Aaron was gone.

Holly felt such fury inside. But then she remembered the voice that said, "You can have your child for eight years, and then he will be restored." *Restored,* of course, means that he came back to us, perfectly normal.

❦   ❦   ❦

You have an expression: "You can't take it with you." Oh no? Yet anything that you love and care about, which brings beauty, can come with you after death. You can manifest it again.

Here is the story of Millie Gumwater, which gives you a small example of Azna's caring.

Millie Gumwater

The other day, a woman with the funny name of Millie Gumwater came to the Other Side, so distraught. She was exactly 102 years old when she died in Macon, Georgia. She had lived in a little shack down by the river and fed every cat, dog, and stray child that walked by. She was truly a light. Her light was so bright along the river bank that every guide who wandered through the area could see it. When she came over, she was so cute—she knew exactly where she was.

As she came down the tunnel, she walked with such a crippled gait. As she came closer to the light, she started to run! It is wonderful to watch them run, their hair turning from silver to gold, lips that were pale and wrinkled turning red; eyes that were blind with cataracts turning blue or whatever color they want to assimilate. She stood there wearing this beautiful pink-and-blue-sashed gingham dress, wringing her hands.

Her guide went over to her and said, "Mildred, what's wrong?" She said, "I couldn't bring my band." We came to find out that this was a ring with a tiny woven band of flowers that her grandmother had given her when she was a child; it no longer fit her finger well, but it did fit to just about the first knuckle on her right hand. She always kept one hand fluttering over this little ring, which caressed her arthritic hand. It was the only possession she'd ever had in life that was worth anything. It was the only thing that no matter how poor she got, she would not sell.

Another guide said, "Reproduce it," but Millie would not hear of that. We told her that on the Other Side, everyone can create thought-forms that are just the same as reality. We said, "We can draw it, make it, and it will appear on your finger," but she said, "It's not the same."

She told us that one flower had been rubbed off. It was a combination of pink, white, and yellow gold, combined to make little interwoven daisy flowers. Every gold- and silversmith came and said, "We can reproduce it. We will scan it. We will look at it closely." They had the scanners out and made it immediately. She would not have it, which is so out of sync with everything we know. But to show you the miracles that can be wrought, someone thought to go to Azna with this. One person said, "Do not go to Her with this silly thing," but another said, "Yes, do it."

Azna is very approachable, so finally someone said, "The heck with it, I'm going," and went up to Azna as She was flouncing through. The guide told her about our problems with Millie, and Azna said, "Then go down and get it." The guide said, "We cannot do that. We cannot disturb the reality that is there." She said, "You cannot? Why not?"

To show you how much we think we know even on my side, I had thought that we'd always been more or less told that we could not disturb the sequence of events on Earth. I always felt that if you entered that atmosphere to displace something, you might have an adverse effect. But we were always living under that idea that we could not disturb time, could not disturb and move objects very much. We know that earthbounds do this, but that was always a disruption of space. We all stood there white-faced and frightened even though She had given us the word.

So with one great flounce, Azna was gone and back with the ring on Her finger to the knuckle. She handed it to Mildred Gumwater, and Millie is the happiest entity in heaven tonight. The moral of this story is that everything can be changed in heaven or in your hell!

ê   ê   ê

O God,

Time is the great healer of grief, deceit, and adversity.
Is it not also the enemy of beauty, and perhaps love?

To ensure constancy in what is really beauty and love,
One must commit oneself totally to the cause, the core.

This, O God, must be the true formula—giving and loving;
If not, then all dreams and hopes are fleeting and illusive.

True constancy lies in You—and Your eternal time.

— Sylvia

ò ò ô ê ê ê

Part II

CREATION

§ Chapter 6 §

THE NATURE OF CREATION

Francine: I am going to discuss Creation and how you wended your way to this planet and why you came. The universe is more vast than you could ever imagine. It has not only height and width, but a tremendous depth that no telescope could ever reach. It is gigantic. The Milky Way would be nothing more than a capillary or freckle—a tiny part of an awesome entity.

In the very "beginning," there was an energy force that was all love and all consciousness, but not in a form. All of us on the Other Side, all of you on your side, and all the beings that inhabit the other dimensions were part of this gigantic swirling mass. That gigantic intelligence began to splinter off, and yet a great deal of the mass remained. The part of it that splintered off was the emotional part. All these fragmented lights, which were all of us, began to descend down into planetary systems. You have all lived on other planets. You have gone through the whole galactic format gathering up knowledge and feelings. This is the first time in the history of this planet that there have been so many different galactic sparks gathered together on one planet, all converging on what we call the last outpost.

You decided to come here because you wanted to perfect more than other entities did. This is the last planet to be won for good. Please! I do not want to give you the feeling that everything on this planet is evil, but this is the planet of thickest negativity. Through all the galaxy, it is known as "the marshes." So all of you who decided to come here really had to be evolved enough to make it. Even your dreams are more bizarre on this planet. It really is true. If there is any psychedelic trip you are on, this is one. This planet is more surreal than any of the others. The medicine is far below par. The intelligence of the whole planet is far below par. This is not negating any of you. It is just that when you come into this one planet, there is a dulling of the mind. That is why so many times you feel that the knowledge is trying to get in, but cannot—the atmospheric conditions are thicker here.

People on other planetary systems have a much easier time communicating with those on the Other Side. People communicate and go into trance to get information as readily as if they were getting a cup of coffee with a friend. The knowledge is that accessible. Eventually, this planet will evolve to approximate this, but not totally. This is the toughest schoolhouse that you will ever be in.

You physically exist within God's silhouette (see Chapter 2), which is the universe. Outside of this, nothing but a vacuum exists. The Other Side of this planet is much like all the others, but this planet is more like an orientation center. That does not mean that people who have passed away do not work, build, or do research, but it is not a forever Other Side. Most of those here on my side are waiting to come in to life or waiting for loved ones to come back. When the period of your Earth years is over, the Other Side of this planet diminishes, and most of you go to a giant, conglomerate Other Side.

Every planet evolves the same way. But due to its stupidity, your planet must evolve and evolve and evolve. On most planets, once people have learned about inquisitions and horrifying things that happen, they never happen again. Your planet has a tendency to have inquisitions, revolutions, holocausts, and the like. But in a way, that is very beneficial, because without all these negative pressures, you would not have accelerated as fast. So you can look at each other and know that you are messengers bringing faith to the world, without feeling ostentatious.

Consciousness must raise in order for this planet to be "saved," as you might say. There is no such thing as "lost," but let us just say *saved,* meaning that everybody perfects. If not, it would be a waste, and that is why so many of you have decided to come in and why the population is running over so badly. Everyone wants to find truth; the real truth that they know is in the very core of their being. Unfortunately, they have a part-truth and that is why cults form such as those led by Jim Jones or Charles Manson. Individuals want a chunk of the truth—certainly it can be gained through classes and knowledge, but the greatest knowledge comes from your own infusion.

How can we get infusion?

You go to Council. This body of advanced entities can counsel and help us. The Council advises people on making their life's chart a reality; they ensure that it will fulfill their chosen goals. They ask us if we choose to go higher or to test something. They govern the Other Side rather than yours. That is why people get aggravated at Council on your level, but they really have nothing to do with this level of life. Our side has a whole political structure. I do not mean politics as you know it—we have a group of loving, governing entities.

You have not even realized the power that you can touch within yourself. You do not realize that you are creators of health and well-being. You are always looking above yourself, and rightly so, because there is a giant intelligence that rules all of us, but if you start thinking of yourself as a spark of the Creator, you may find that you can accomplish more things than you ever realized. The reason you stop is that society or religion or culture says you cannot attain those heights. You look at someone who has, and you say, "That is fine for them, but not for me." So somewhere along the line, you "cash in" your chips—but there is no end to your potential and no end to the power that you contain. Oh yes, you can create negativity, but I will tell you what will happen if you do: You will be destroyed by it. If you send poison darts to someone else—for example, if you create a satanic cult or any kind of mental deviation that is malicious in intent—then the only one ever hit by the dart is you, no one else.

Do not be so scrupulous about your thoughts. "Thoughts are

things," as they say, but know that you are human. Your words should not be so monitored by you. I do not mean that you can maliciously hurt others, but if you really ask God for help so that your words should only be truth, you do not have to worry about monitoring. If you know why you feel the way you do, it is easier to handle. Most of you suffer with life, and it is more terminal than any disease. Yet no one ever gives you a diagnosis for it. You think you are alone and isolated in your feelings and anxieties. You are tired out from the journey and the lives you have lived, tired of taking yourself from one part of the universe to the other trying to make many, many people who are not evolved listen to your words and listen to the belief you have that you can heal yourself—to listen to your belief that all power resides in you. It becomes very tiring.

Health

Care about your body; it is the temple in which your soul resides. It is good to care about your appearance. Make sure your hair shines and your clothes are clean, because this mirrors what your soul feels. I do not mean just one day when you've had no time to groom yourself. Notice a person going through severe depression over a period of time: Their hair and eyes get dull, their clothing seems just thrown together, and their posture is slouched down with a bowed head. The whole physical vehicle begins to show the manifestation within the soul.

Let me tell you an interesting thing. You have always heard the word *sanctuary,* have you not, or *chapel?* The ancients knew that a sanctuary or any place that had been blessed or domed, such as the Ark of the Covenant, was a sacred place. You can certainly make a sanctuary and a blessed place within your own home. I am sure that in your house there is a certain room that you love more. I would ask you to get something like a relic or a candle to make that place a sanctuary—not because that object has any power, but only because of what it represents. It helps manifest white entities around you; they see what you are doing and begin to push out darkness.

Health has nothing to do with having brand-new clothes; rather, it is as if the paint is beginning to peel on a house, or there are weeds in the yard. You begin to feel that the inhabitant does not care anymore. To care only about the soul, and not the body, is a ridiculous, passive attitude—a waste! Why would you have picked something in which to reside if you were only going to make it defective? Let me tell you about what certain substances do to your body. Be *very* careful of your own soul's evolvement, not because of "sin," but watch your consumption of drugs, pills, and alcohol. They dull your wits and your senses, and you will not be able to function spiritually.

There are so many nutrients, so many types of food you can take into your body that will not cause you to behave erratically. We have found that almost every entity who comes into life becomes dependent on or addicted to something. There is no person who is not addicted to something—perhaps only a color, certain likes and dislikes, or religious beliefs. What I would say to you is this: "Moderation in all things!" Also, pick something that will not disturb your mental processes—something with which you can still function. Alcohol, especially wine, is one of the worst poisons you can take in because of the bacteria, sediment, and fermentation. It is not like the old wines, which were fermented in huge kegs. The process that is used now is poisonous. I am saying this from a health standpoint.

Seek for the Truth

Do not settle for anything that you cannot understand. Everything that you want to know might be difficult for the human mind, but there is an answer. Withholding answers is a control factor. You were told in religions and secret societies that you were not supposed to know everything or you were not able to understand it. That is all foolishness; nothing is so mysterious that you cannot ask for and receive an answer. What I am telling you, in essence, is that you have a very high peak to climb. You are going to reach the top. When you are walking toward a peak, you think you are never going to reach it, but you will!

I am convinced that within your heart of hearts, or as they say in ancient religions, your *touchstone,* you will be very aware when truths are spoken!

ॐ ॐ ॐ

*"I incorporate God into everything, because
God is everything to me."*

— Sylvia

ॐ ॐ ॐ ॐ ॐ ॐ

$ Chapter 7 $

SEVEN SCHEMATICS

Sylvia: The schematics are only a way for our finite minds to under-stand creation. This knowledge always resided in the mind of God. But again, for our finite minds, we are going to itemize, from one to seven, the major aspects of the universe that we live in.

First Schematic—Creation of the Universe

The creation of the universe is the totality of God; it encompass-es God and *is* God. Contained within it are all the planetary systems with life possible on many, many planets. This resists the Big Bang theory and goes along with the belief that everything was immediate-ly set into motion. The first premise is that it was always there.

Everything in the universe was made ready through the evolution, rotation, and orbiting of the planets. Each solar system had its own sun, and each planet swung into place to be readied for life, far enough away from the sun, having a moon for gravitational pull for the oceans. Each planet was prepared, whether it was by an ice age or a volcanic age, for human life on it.

Then colonization, of course, especially for Earth's life, came from other planets. But we have to get back to the original planet or planets in which there was a direct infusion of entities who were put onto a planet, or some planetary system, by God, and were immediately able to procreate. These entities, we are told, were created in tube-like objects emanating from the Godhead, and they eventually became flesh when they incarnated.

The first schematic prepared the planetary systems for entities to have a place in which to incarnate.

Francine: The question, "Am I an old soul?" is meaningless. Everyone is as old as each other. If you are referring semantically to how many lifetimes you have had, then that is another thing entirely. But everyone, in fact, is just as old as everyone else. There were not a few souls who were projected out, and then eons later a whole new bunch came out. No! It all happened simultaneously, in a big bang, as it were.

There was an eternity in which we were not manifested as individual entities, but yet we were these molecular souls. We were not in a spiritual, glorified form for that eternity. We are now in the seventh eternity schematic. The schematics go in circular forms. The eternity is complete within itself. In the beginning, there was always the Uncreated Mass. Think of yourself as tiny balls of light containing the total you, but not yet in a spiritual, glorified form. It is like an egg, and yet it was a thinking being. It really does not matter whether you are a ball or a tube, because the totality of you stays. Once we were spewed forth in these cylindrical shapes, we came in like cocoons. We peeled off from each other and went about in the reincarnation schematic. Going to other planets in glorified bodies was one schematic.

I myself have had only one Earth life, but I have had many lives on other planetary systems. I do not want to come down into this Earth life. Going back to the Other Side and working is itself a schematic, as is migrating to other planets, or choosing to go back into the molecular state. From what I understand, most entities do not want to go back into the Uncreated Mass—not because it is bad, but only because they like the merging and the glorious feeling of your soul having arms and legs and eyes.

Second Schematic—Creation of Entities

Sylvia: The second act was the creation of entities, although it's true that all these schematics happened simultaneously. Entities were created as individual parts of God, like separate sparks emanating from the Divine Sparkler. These were the feminine or emotional side, experiencing for God. All these entities were conceived at the same time—their minds, bodies, and spirits. Each entity's level of knowledge was very important and equal—at the same level from the beginning. Of course, as each life progressed, they did start to differ in terms of spiritual evolvement, because we each evolve to our own level of knowledge. But for this schematic, all entities were on the same level.

Here in the second schematic is where "dark" entities began to separate from the light. From the very "beginning," a fluke developed—yet it was "always" there for us to learn from. All entities were created perfectly without the concept of evil instilled; however, the dark entities, from the very point of creation, chose to separate from the Godhead.

Francine: Please understand that this concept of light and dark entities has absolutely nothing to do with skin color. This has to do with the soul. The color of the skin has nothing to do with the soul's color.

Sylvia: Certain groups of entities were created with more knowledge so that they could perform special missions or functions, such as Jesus, the master teachers, Council, the Archetypes, and other leaders. They are all equal in their elevated understanding.

Also, entities were created in duality as male and female soulmates. Everything in God is repeated, just as God has male and female sides. We cannot negate the Mother God aspect—She created females just as the static side of God created males. On this planet, the feminine side is dominant, because it is the emotional, experiencing side.

Soulmates evolve separately and revolve back toward each other, finally reaching each other near the end of their evolvement. Most of the time, entities do not come down with their soulmate; it is very rare. Most of the time, one soulmate stays on the Other Side and watches out for the entity that is in life, just as a spirit guide does.

Third Schematic—Placement on Planets

A location with changing environments was needed for created entities to reside in while experiencing for God. Of course, this is covered somewhat in the first schematic with the creation of the universe. This need for changing environments bears up the Biblical book of Genesis, which states that Adam lived in a perfect environment and then was pushed out so that he could toil and suffer and know the difference between good and evil.

It is interesting to note, since so much of the Bible is symbolic, that eating from the Tree of Knowledge meant that you must go into life to experience that knowledge. Eating of the Tree of Life is not enough. Once you have bitten into knowledge, you must experience it. So a location was needed to find oneself, to experience everything from death to life—all the problems, heartache, and joy.

Fourth Schematic—Creation of Other Dimensions

Because physical death is a reality, a location was needed for the real spiritual body. An "Other Side" surrounds each inhabited planet for the long-lasting residence of created entities. It is an environment of love and peace without "death," where awareness and knowledge are heightened and one evolves intellectually and lovingly with the "veil" lifted. As St. Paul says, "We see through a mirror darkly."

Other dimensions are nothing more than the Other Side. Each planet that contains life has its own Other Side. Eventually, as entities accumulate evolvement at the final schematic, all the Other Sides merge together.

Fifth Schematic—Reincarnation

Some entities evolve faster than others, showing the individuality of each. Because some did not evolve completely with one life, God gave His created entities the opportunity to live more than once, gaining experience and evolving according to a great plan that shows His love and mercy. Each entity, with their own theme, will experience a given number of lives, as many as they choose. Lives are written by the person and chosen specifically for their life theme, which is the purpose for which they came down to perfect. So a certain theme may be any one of the 45 that are possible, such as Builder, Experiencer, Activator, Tolerance, Patience, and so on.

An entity will go through the chosen number of lives until they get to a point where they know they have completed that theme to the best of their ability. Entities then go to the Other Side and, of course, keep on working and giving homage to God whether it is in research or orientation of in- and outgoing entities, which is nothing more than entities coming into and going out of life.

Sixth Schematic—Incarnating on Other Planets

Reincarnation on other planets is also possible to gain a "new" type of experience. Some entities cannot experience enough from just one planet, although we are told that this planet is one of the hardest. Francine has always called it "the insane asylum of the universe." Some of us, due to our charted plan, will not only come to this planet, but will, by our own choice, incarnate in other environments to enhance our lives—possibly to be helpers to other entities—in order to evolve and gain a greater scope of knowledge.

This planet's negativity, we are told, makes us learn faster. Nevertheless, we have found through our vast knowledge of regressive techniques that some entities, after this life or even between or before it, have been on other planetary systems to learn.

Seventh Schematic—All of Creation Merges

In the final schematic, all creations will live in perfect harmony, love, and peace. This also goes along with the fourth schematic, in which the other dimensions will finally be cemented together. Constant knowledge will be obtained about God and will circle back to Him.

ፄ ፄ ፄ

Francine: Knowledge that is advanced, very spiritual, deep, and theological in essence is sometimes too much for some hearts to bear, and that is a shame. Some people are not ready to learn, absorb, or go on to the next level. Those who are enlightened burn with the fire of enthusiasm; they cannot wait until the next chapter of the book, until the next knowledge comes.

All this is in the Akashic Records, and if I could, I would transport all of us there, but unfortunately I cannot because you are in human bondage, literally. You are bound to this earth more than any earth-bound spirit could ever be. You labor with your feet of clay. I know because I very well remember my life from 1500 to 1519, and certainly coming into Sylvia's body brings back the whole morphic resonance of just how tiresome and miserable it is to be in a human body.

Once you have been let loose from that human bondage, a euphoria encompasses you, and you will experience a spiraling clearness of thought and be freed from all addictions. I do not just mean drinking, drugs, or such things, but the addictions of having to be somewhere at a certain time, or not being able to answer only to yourself, God, and the people that you choose to have around you. What you feel, once again, is truly the morphic resonance of this miracle called "dying." You always refer to the miracle of birth. That is not a miracle; it is a penance! The miracle of death, where the soul transcends and becomes as light as a feather floating or zooming or running through the tunnel, as most of you will do—this is the true miracle.

After you have lived your life, you come back to the Other Side.

You go down the tunnel and are absolutely aware that there is no fear! You go directly to the Hall of Wisdom, a beautiful domed building with a huge crystal on top through which rosy half-light shines as it rotates. The Hall of Wisdom is a place in which your guide and you sit down and look at a scanning apparatus by which you can go through your life. You have heard the expression, "My whole life flashed in front of my eyes"—many people right before death really trip into these scanning mechanisms. No one but you sits and watches. There is no judgmental voice saying, "You really were bad here." No. You sit and view your life, with your guide or alone, whichever the choice may be. Many times people flag certain parts of their lives to show their friends later. There is constant researching.

You will see groups sitting around, viewing parts of a person's life and talking to each other about what could have been done to better help that individual's spirituality. Everything is done without ego. You do not see people standing up and justifying their position. They are truly interested in how they could have done it better. All this is personal, so it does not have to be taken out into the open arena unless you wish it to be.

No one puts your life on display on the screen and holds you up for ridicule. That would never need to be done anyway. There is no one who ridicules you any more than *you* do! This is one thing you must come to believe. There are not many such truths, but for your own spirituality, you *must* know that you do not have a judging God. He cannot and will not be; He is a loving God who does not judge. God is made of wisdom and love.

Many times, when a person comes over, there will be a group of people that will sit and want to merge with that person to experience their life without having to do it. I would, however, advise you not to merge with Sylvia right away, because some of her experiences have been so horrendous that you could blow apart. I am serious about that!

In *Man and His Symbols,* Carl Jung states that everything in life, down to the clothes you wear, is a symbol. So why not pull down from the highest order of things? On the Other Side, we still use symbols. It is very smart to reaffirm what you are. Are you a lion, an ant, or a beautiful gazelle? Are you a sapling, an oak, or a spindly little fir tree? It is wonderful to affirm. In all affirmations, a symbol of life is used to make the cells well. "I will be well; I believe in God; God is almighty; God is pure; I am pure."

For a powerful example, consider the symbols used by Carl Simonton in cancer research of black knights fighting white knights. In human form, you need symbols. The mind cannot attach to ethereal substances. No. Of course you do not have to, but it is just easier if you do. Without symbols, you cannot affirm or do affirmations.

Can we enlighten everyone?

No! Stupidity cannot be enlightened, nor can greed or avarice. Those who close their ears will not hear us. Hopefully some of you will pray hard enough so that some people with thick skullcaps on their heads will be enlightened. That could mean your family, your friends, or people that are close. If they are not enlightened, then you keep your crown chakra open so that you receive the Light.

This may mean that you have to leave people behind—even loved ones, or those you thought were loved ones, or family and friends with whom you cannot get along—then you will be called. Many times people did not understand when Jesus said, "Drop it all and follow me." He did not mean himself; he meant the wisdom that he brought.

Option Life

An option life is like extra credit in school; it is for when you want extra advancement. This is Sylvia's option life, so please look at her and reconsider whether you want to do one. They can be horrendous because they are the result of somebody volunteering and asking for everything to happen, to become an example for everyone else. That is like going into a lion's den without a whip. I would not advise anyone to come into an option life because you really do not have any sides on you at all—you are just up for grabs. It's like going deep-sea diving and not having any gear on: horrendous and deadly!

What happens with so many of you, because you took an option life down here, is that I think you are up for grabs for whatever anybody wants to throw at you, which happens many times with very spiritual, elevated entities. In other words, you come down with no holds barred. Anybody can do anything they want to you because they know you are an elevated entity. The only thing that we are terribly afraid of is that the white entities come down into this nightmare and sometimes get scarred; then we really have to make sure their essence is not too battered. We have to cocoon them, because a white entity will never be lost. But they are in danger of being scarred.

You are never going to scar a dark entity. You cannot. But you can damage the essence of a white entity. The essence gets scarred, and it takes a long time to make that person all right. It takes a long time to regain their full essence. It is very similar to what happens when a person on your side has a nervous breakdown. They become so maligned, bruised, and hurt that we cannot get them to stick together right. Persecution, hurt, and wrongdoing have scarred them.

For instance, when Joan of Arc came over, we almost did not get her back. It was so horrific! When white entities take that kind of battering through many lives, their essence can get scarred trying to prove a belief system such as Gnosticism. That does not mean we do not eventually get them back, but we think it is a shame. It is like white knights going into battle. It's so important to make the connection—to love each other, to hold and heal each other. There is nothing that salves the soul any more than touching, healing, doing for, nurturing, petting, and loving. If you do not have that, you have no singular way to ever recuperate some of the essence lost.

Now you may say, "I do not have anybody who lives with me, strokes me, or cares about me." Then come and hug each other—in church, in here, in your classes, or wherever you are. Hug each other, heal each other, touch each other.

You must realize that being in a last life is very prominent for you. It is very deep and very serious; there is no longer any place for curiosity. When you finish your Earthly life and are going back through the tunnel, many of you will choose option lives on other planets. Most of you may say at this point, "I do not want to do that." Please note the word *option*. Even though an option life is very precarious, it is also very rewarding as far as spiritual accumulation and progressing further on the Other Side.

You may ask, "Why would you want to progress further, if in any position you are just as happy?" It is because the capacity for happiness is greater; the increasing love in this state of bliss is something that everyone wishes for and aspires to. It's like saying, "I am so in love that I don't think I could be happier." Yet something comes along and makes you happier still. Once you reach that height or have touched it, you want more.

Are there other Gnostic groups?

Very few. There is one in the Basque community that is coming in, and another in South America; they are springing up now in little bits and pieces. Be very careful about what people say Gnosticism is. Read about it and find out the truth. It is now becoming a buzzword.

I think it is more important now to form a Circle of Light. The summer and winter solstices and the spring and fall equinoxes are the most powerful days of the year. They bring about the most grace. That is when Azna shines Her mantle of Light on every person. Believe me, She is very picky. You might not like to believe that the Goddess does this, but you see, emotion has its likes and dislikes. She does play favorites. She responds mostly to the love of Her—She then loves back. That has nothing to do with male or female. That is how emotion works.

When did we choose to be Gnostics?

Oh, you picked it way back. Most of you picked it many times. It has started and failed many times. You would all get together, then wander off when it became too difficult. Gnosticism is very difficult. It has very, very faint outlines. And yet as you get into it more, you realize that the outline becomes very concrete and clear. It looks like it is very blended on the outside, but once you get into it, then it begins to be a really harsh and individual trip for the soul.

Everyone that really is a seeker after their own truth is a Gnostic. And here is an amazing insight about that—Sylvia was talking to a marvelous Persian man the other day who said, "It does not matter, does it, what we call God?" She said, "Of course not. God is one God whether you call Him Joe, Allah, Charlie, or whatever. It is all the same God."

ɤ ɤ ɤ

Let others defy You and say You're not there.
Let them toss You aside without any care.

Let the scholars expound on You day after day;
Let the scientists confuse and obliterate what You say.

Let them all try to find You in a tree or a dove;
But You and I know that You are . . . simply Love.

— Sylvia

ᛞ ᛞ ᛞ ᛞ ᛞ ᛞ

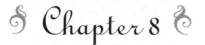

Chapter 8

TWELVE LEVELS OF THE SOUL

Francine: This discussion about the 12 levels of the soul is probably one of the most significant and most in-depth that we have had. Not to brag, but I am one of the few entities who has been trained in this doctrine about the formation of the soul. It is not written anywhere, even in the Urantia or the Dead Sea Scrolls.

The 12 levels of the soul are nothing more than an explanation of the seven schematics—they discuss why we came in and what we are experiencing for. That is the overview, more or less, of your course of study.

This first course of study involves the beginnings of Creation and how it all started, past lives and how they relate to what is going on, how one ultimately perfects through them, how one can get in touch with them, and how one life applies to other lives as a morphic resonance.

In this discussion, we will go into them very extensively, as well as the whole pattern of where souls go in other planetary places, what the advancement is, what the very beginnings of some souls were, and where they came from.

The First Level—Thought-Forms in the Mind of God

The first level of the soul has to do with the creative impulses. This subject is very—I will not say *laborious*—but very *deep* theologically. This is the very root of the most ancient and authentic beliefs about where we came from. We have always said that from the very "beginning," we always were. Now that you are advanced enough, you must realize that you were not always in the form you are in now. You did always exist in the mind of God as the first phase of your soul. There was an individual synaptic spark in God's mind that formed a specific, clear-cut thought or particle of His being that you came from. Now, imagine if every thought that you thought of any concrete "nowness" became a creation. You would have quite a conglomerate. That is why for so many years you have heard that "thoughts are things." They are, especially in the mind of God.

Sylvia: In this level, we were always a reality within the mind of God as exact thought-forms—always thought of, always omnipresent, since God is the Prima Mobilae, the Unmoved Mover, and so are we. It is hard to speak about "alwaysness" because it is disruptive for the human mind to comprehend. When we say, "You will always be," that is not a problem. But when we say, "You always were," that is a problem. You say, "What do you mean, I always was?" You have to think of a circle.

It must be that we always were because if God had *suddenly* thought of you one day, then God is imperfect, and that cannot be possible. So we believe in the perfection of God who is all-knowing and all-loving—and so we always were within that perfection.

The Second Level—The Word Made Flesh

Francine: When God began to have these synaptic impulses or creative thoughts in His alwaysness, then the second level of the soul's maturity was put into being. Now, what I mean is that the thought was made flesh. On the Other Side, you became an entity.

That is, you came into being—but at this point you were only half-formed.

You contained the sum total of what you were and what you would be, but without experience. So you were very much like lumps of clay, each having separate shapes and colors, so to speak, but unformed. But nevertheless, in this piece of clay was a heart with feeling and sensitivity, and there began to be the imprint of the theme that was to evolve.

Sylvia: As the sparks came off the Divine Sparkler—as we emanated from the Divine Force—we began to embark on our perfection schemes. You know within your own mind that we are miniature gods. For years people have had such a horror of saying that, thinking it is the ultimate blasphemy. But really, it's just like saying, "Aren't you the daughter of so-and-so?"

We have always been part of God's lineage; therefore, we have God's genetics. We've always heard that we were made in the image and likeness of God, but when we say that we *are* God, everybody is shocked. Why do we not carry the thought outward—not belief, but rational thought? As we began to emanate from the Divine, we were thought. We are now the individual spark that came off, totally intact and in contact with our Source.

Francine: There are so many entities that are not advanced enough to comprehend this point. It should make you very proud that you have advanced this far. But in the beginning, everyone had more or less the same aptitudes and abilities. How they used them and how they accelerated is part of their spirituality.

For example, some people came with heightened intelligence and never did anything with it; we think of that as an entity who did not choose to evolve. That is all right. They stay at their very base level. We all know entities like that, on both your side and mine. That is not a criticism, just a fact. They do not choose to work at it. Other entities may be lazy in the first part of their lives, like children in school, then they suddenly get bitten by the bug of education and want to excel. It's an individual thing. The thought processes are very individualistic. That has to be so, because all the conglomerate sparks make up the whole. Yes, everybody was born with the same basis from the very beginning.

In the "beginning," all of us were more like the intellectual side of God—very static, concrete, and unmovable, but with certain determinations. In the second phase, you became an entity with the beginnings of what you were going to do. You began to decide whether you were going to incarnate or not and how many incarnations you might have, and you began to have a sketchy program of what you wanted to fulfill, more or less, like a lesson plan.

The Third Level—Developing Your Theme

The third level of the soul is the outline and program of our planned evolvement. Now you began to develop your theme, and chart out your course of action. Much like a writer begins to sketch out chapters, you began to outline the chapters of your life. This chapter will be action-packed, this one will be experiencing, this one will be an example, this one tolerance, this one rejection, and so on.

Sylvia: Here, we began to write our charts. Every time I say that, a little part of my brain goes, "Oh, no! Could I have been so stupid on the Other Side—idiotic, insane, and retarded enough—to sit down and write this nightmare with so many dark nights of the soul?" Of course you did, because you were *smart*. If you write, "I am going to be beautiful, wonderful, and wealthy; everyone will love me, and I am going to have everything," it would not add to your perfection. Only when the metal is tempered can you form it into something. Only when the gold has been fired does it become a ring. Otherwise, it is a lump. What is a diamond? A coal lump. But keep it heated and under pressure, then chisel and work with it, and it becomes magnificent and brilliant. That is what we are—our soul is a diamond waiting to be uncovered.

So the tougher and more daring we are, the more experience we write in. But as we spend time in the physical body, we find that life is harder than expected. On the Other Side, it's wonderful—we wrote a chart thinking, "This is great. I will take this and that, whatever," because it is so pleasant over there. Then we come down here and say, "Oh, *no!*" Have you ever looked into a baby's eyes? They have that look, "Oh, no. Here I am again!" But the goal is perfection. So, as we wrote our chart, we began to figure out what we were going to accomplish in every life.

Francine: You also charted for lives on various planets. For example, 38 lives on one planet, 14 on another, or whatever you wanted it to be. Some will finish at 62, or maybe 28 lives. Many Gnostic entities come from Nuvo and only chose to come to this planet for so many lives, because this is the toughest one.

The Fourth Level—Writing Your Chart

The fourth level is where you decided what you were ultimately going to accomplish. Now it becomes more definitive. After making the outline of your chapters, you begin to write a very definitive script about what you want to accomplish in each given life. In level three, the labels at the top were very broad. If you had the theme of Tolerance, then in the fourth level you decided which aspects of life to tolerate—poverty in one life, having no legs in the next, then great wealth, the kidnaping of a child, and so on.

Sylvia: At the fourth level, each life's details are filled in. We took a theme, and we are going to perfect it as best we can in every life. Some themes seem tougher than others, but we cannot always say that. A Humanitarian theme, to someone shy, might be harder than for someone like me. So the theme rubs differently on every single person. Of course, the relationship to the theme and the experiencing factor for that person makes it even stronger.

Your experience is a direct feedback to God, Who, in all knowingness, cannot experience except through His "ten fingers." We are those fingers that move and experience. Not that we do not have intelligence, but we are experiencing for God because we are sparks of the Divine. That is such an uplifting thought! You will never get lost in the milieu of things. You are never going to go somewhere that you will not be noticed. As Jesus said, "Every hair on your head is numbered." Can you tell me that parents do not know the love between their children and them in Earthly life? How do you think that compares to the love between Father and Mother God and Their offspring? It is even more magnificent because of Their magnanimousness and gigantic ability to love. Imagine what Their love must be like!

Does our theme change on other planets?

Francine: Yes. Your theme only applies to this planet. Also, when a soul gets to its last life, the themes all converge. That is why people on their last life have a hard time putting themselves into one particular theme. They will pick up smatterings of them all.

After we incarnate, can we modify our chart?

We have drawn it up, but we can certainly program for modification. We can, as Sylvia says, "have a fender-bender rather than a head-on collision." We are not discrediting Azna—She is the only one who can intercept to eradicate or change the chart. Time frames can speed up or slow down. As much as we rage against our chart, asking why this or that did not happen, the fact of the matter is that this has nothing to do with negative blocks. It only has to do with the fact that you made yourself delay things, but your dreams will ultimately come true.

The Fifth Level—Beginning to Experience

The fifth level is interesting. This is where you began to separate from the intellect and go into emotion. Before this you were pure thought, reason, and logic. Why? Because you had not experienced. You were more like Adam was before he bit into the fruit of knowledge, as described in Genesis 3. Pure knowledge, without experience, must of course leave the Garden of Eden and go into life to experience. That is really what Genesis means when it says that humankind was tossed out of paradise. It is absolutely beautiful because it spells it out in perfect metaphorical language. No one can learn everything by just grabbing knowledge. We must go down and experience it. Thank God, literally—it is necessary to experience the emotional side of yourself. The Archetypes, although beautiful and wonderful, are pure intellect. That is why they stand as guardian sentinels of the soul, but have no emotion. If you are ever going to call on an Archetype, do so for protection or stability. You cannot call on them for emotion because they have never lived a life.

It is impossible to ever find anyone in human form, alien or not, who does not have an emotional side. You may deny this and say to me, "But a person I know has *absolutely* no emotion." You are wrong. They have only masked that emotion behind an exterior. That is probably the sickest thing one can do to a soul—to mask emotion behind the guise of intelligence. It is tremendously draining for someone to keep up a facade of constant linear mind with no emotion. This is an emotional planet, and emotion is the impetus by which everything gets done. And yet, what have you been told? "Emotion is bad; people should not be so emotional." Without that emotion you cannot live, experience, and perfect.

Sylvia: The fifth level is knowledge starting to experience; it is emotion beginning to separate from pure intellect. That is where our heart and solar plexus begin to hurt. This is the tough level, where you separate yourself from the giant intellect.

When you eat of the Tree of Knowledge, it means that you have to go down and experience. Do you not see how rational that is? God said, "Once you eat of knowledge, you have to know the whole scope." Everybody said, "Oh boy, Eve sure was nasty. Wasn't she awful?" But she was nothing more than the symbol of emotion. She had to be the driving force for intellect, because intellect by itself can do nothing. If, for example, I conceive of this book, I still need the impetus to make it a reality. Something has to be the mover.

The Sixth Level—Incarnating into Physical Lives

In the sixth phase, you began to incarnate into physical lives. Here, we knew that we were going to separate from home and have homesickness from that. We spend all of our lives homesick. Do not say otherwise. You can sublimate it, saying, "I need a car; I need a house; I need Mr. or Mrs. Right," but it is more than that. It is a deep wanting to go home. That does not mean we are going to take an exit by committing suicide. No, we cannot do that because then we will have to come back immediately and do it all over again, the exact same thing you were trying to escape from. Here we are always a little bit separate. On the Other Side we all merge with each other. If I want to share your thoughts, then I flow into you, you flow into me— we come into each other. We cannot do that in life. I don't care how close you get sexually or how much you can hold your baby tight, or how much you love—you cannot get close enough to a human being, because the physical body separates you.

Anyway, the sixth level—incarnation into the physical world—is the toughest. It was always known that the only way we were ever going to perfect was in a negative environment, because you are not going to perfect in a happy, wonderful one. This does not mean that life is not wonderful. Regardless of what has ever happened to me in my life, I have really always had a good time. My grandmother used to say, "Sylvia, if ignorance is bliss, you would be a whole blister." Tomorrow is always a better day; it is always going to be okay, happier, just fine. That is what saved me. That does not mean I have not had pain, but I did see better days. I keep saying to myself, "This too will pass." Toothaches, childbirth, divorces, hurts, the IRS—it all passes!

I often wonder what I was thinking about when I was picking my human body. We actually choose our physical body, even though it is defective. The physical body decays. Anything that is transitory is defective. So you say, "Why didn't I pick a better one than this?! Why wasn't I shorter, taller, heavier, lighter?" That in itself is something that we must overcome in the physical world. We spend so much time worrying about our nose, our eyes, our hair—then we get older and die, and who cares? I don't think anybody is going to remember the fact that your eyes were too small or your nose was too big or your whatever else was too large or small. Do you know what they will remember? What you did with your life. What your soul did to touch theirs.

I love to tell the children's story (since I was a schoolteacher for so many years) about the little girl who couldn't find her mother. She ran through a crowd, screaming, "You have to know what my mother looks like. She is the most beautiful woman in the village," and everybody was frantic. They thought, *Who is this woman?* The little girl said, "I am telling you, she is the *most beautiful* woman. You will know her immediately." So everybody is looking for this beautiful woman. Nobody could find her. Then, all of a sudden, out of the crowd came this snaggle-toothed, straggly-haired, babushka-clad, short, very round woman. The child looked up, her face shining, and said, "There she is! Don't you see? She is the most beautiful woman in the world." And of course she was, through the eyes of that child.

How many people do we know who appear beautiful, yet the more we get to know them, the more we realize that there is nothing *truly* attractive in them. Or vice versa. It is the *soul* that makes true beauty. So in this physical world, along with renting the body and everything that we have, open up your hand and let it go. This does not mean you have to give it away or that you do not want nice things. Everybody needs certain things, but open up your hand and know that everything is transitory.

We worry about retirement and wills and money, and all of that. Of course, we do not want to be bag people. The nice thing about Gnostics is that they would never let anybody become bag people. They formed communities and took care of everybody. There is something good to be said about that. So at least when we are together, we will all have the same kind of cart with little doves on it. At least we can stand around and talk about the good old days. That is more than most of them have.

The Seventh Level—Dark Entities Manifest

Francine: In the seventh level—and seven is a very powerful number—is where we began to see some entities "slipping through the cracks." After incarnation, some entities began to negate either their emotional or intellectual sides, feeling that they were so evolved that there was nothing beyond themselves. I do not mean that they just denied God, because we have seen atheists who are purely white entities. You might ask, "How can a white entity be atheistic?" Most often, atheists simply do not go along with religious dogma. But you will never really find a true atheist who does not believe in something. They have some god—too often, it is only power, money, or the self.

Here in the seventh level, we began to see entities turning either dark or light, and never turning back. It almost seemed like a trial period that everybody goes through in life, whether you make it or break it. Some could not decide; we call them "gray" entities. They did not know whether to be white or dark, so they chose neither. You see, being gray lets them walk on both sides of the fence. They are a little bad and a little good. You may say, "Well, we are all like that." Not really—they are more destructive. You say, "Well, why are they so good most of the time, but then they did this awful thing?" Gray!

We think, from our research, that it was because the shock of incarnating might have created this in some people who happened to pick a life early on in which they were glorified too quickly. So from the embryonic state, when life was breathed into them and they had all the beauty, intellect, and emotion, perhaps they had a wondrous life as a king or queen or something, and because of that, began to turn wrong.

Sylvia: Everybody had the option to be either dark, gray, or light. The funny thing about it is that if you are white, you will always be white. But the grays said, "Maybe I will worship the materialistic world. I will do anything necessary to get to the top, and step on any-one who gets in my way." That is what was symbolized in the Bible when Jesus was taken to the mountaintop with Satan. "Do you want all this? I can give you all this. I can give you adoration, power, and money." That is not to say that I do not believe in materialism, but to put so much emphasis on it makes the soul gray. It does! It makes you negative; you feel bad and worry too much.

At Creation, was everyone made white?

Francine: In God's mind, yes. When the sparks went out of God's mind as from a Divine Sparkler, at that moment in the second level, each soul decided whether to be dark or white. But while in the mind of God, within the purest form of love, beauty, and righteousness where nothing is tainted, everyone was white. When the thought-forms became flesh and became the experiencing part of God, at that exact moment, each made their decision.

We began to see a parting then and their own separate, as you might say, "union" developing here at the seventh level. Almost like you see in any group that wants to create dissension, you will see a political group begin to form. You get these little groups of ego that begin to separate and create problems.

Are there dark entities on other planets?

Yes, but not like here. Most entities decided that this was the best time to go in order to perfect certain themes. In other words, if you wanted to be an actor, you would go to the Lee Strasberg school, the finest. To be a lawyer, you would go to an Ivy League college. You would go to the best if you really wanted to hone yourself.

White entities, more than any others coming down to this planet, really took on a big mouthful—more than you could chew or swallow. You see, what is so bad about this planet is that it is unchartable. This whole planet has a terrible time being charted, individually and collectively. For example, say you're going to the Amazon. I give you bug spray, a net, shots, and pills, and you are ready. You have your safari hat and suit on and are ready to deal with every possible problem. Then once in the jungle, we find out that all the pills and shots are now obsolete, because there are different strains of viruses for which we have no pills. That is what this planet is like.

You were told specifically when you came down that all bets were off. Any planet with so many dark entities cannot be charted. We knew that we could help you somewhat—we could try to push your canoe a little—but we did not know what kind of rocks would be set up, because this is a dark planet, and dark entities play by their own rules.

God is going to make sure that you perfect. People are constantly saying, "But what if a person just gives up?" The person who gives up would do so anyway. You see, that is what you must realize. You are not going to make anybody dark who is not already dark.

Is being dark irreversible?

Yes—a totally irrevocable decision, except for the gray entities, and those are the ones you have to worry about the most! They can be beguiling and wily because they are indecipherable. There is no discerning exactly what decision they will make at any given time. You cannot track them. The dark ones are easier to track. They are then left to come back into life after life.

Do dark entities have their own Other Side?

Absolutely. They began to form their own political structure. The dark Other Side did not surface until they got into life, when the reincarnation phase started in the sixth level. We believe that the disposition was there, but we did not see it change until the incarnation began to take effect.

It was strange because it seemed to form of itself after we thought that everything had been created. It seems to have been created after everything else. Now some theologians on our side said it was always there, but it was not inhabited. But then, I have to ask the question— they must have thought somebody was going to inhabit it or it would not have been created in the first place. That is only deductive reasoning. So if it was there, they must have known somebody was going to end up there. It should give you great courage and security to realize that you are not one of those who slipped through the cracks.

Are dark entities a slip in God's thinking?

In all thought processes, there is always that possibility, and I am certainly not questioning God because I have such a devotion to our Maker—but God's thought process encompassed everything that humankind could ever think or ever will think, and more. If that is true, then there had to be dark thoughts. Within Om, like your own subconscious, there is a darkness that is not created by Him. Please never feel that. But there is an antithesis to Him that the dark entities represent, very much like a cancer cell.

I do not want to ever make you think that there is anything that had to do with our Maker that was a slip. I do not want to make it ever sound like it was accidental. So I know for a fact, definitively, that God allowed or demanded or put into motion the dark to be an antithesis for us. None of those entities will ever be lost, because eventually they will be absorbed back into the first level.

Can anyone turn dark?

We are convinced that entities who are white could never have been anything else but white. Are we now forced into the feeling of being more blessed by God? I don't think so. I think that everybody had the same chances, but that God knew, although we did not, that we still had the free will to do whatever we pleased at this point. So many chose to slip through the cracks. Everybody started out with a pure, Godlike motive, and what we did with it after that set us into motion.

What is the nature of gray entities?

We really lump them in with the dark. I think I even like the real dark better than the gray. Fence-sitters worry me. At least with the dark you are very aware, almost at first contact, that this person is evil. You do not have to make any decision about what you are going to do. You back up, your hair stands on end, and you feel totally put off and repulsed. Gray entities have a coaxing, almost seductive, maniacal way of pulling you toward them—they are wheedling, hypocritical, and deceptive. They are the most frightening. With the dark, you almost have to admire their dedication, because they are totally committed to themselves. But you never know exactly where you stand with the gray. *They* don't know where they stand. The unfortunate part about this is that far more grays turn black than white.

What is the percentage of black, gray, and white on Earth?

Seventy percent gray and black. Thirty percent white.

What is the purpose of dark entities?

The dark entity is for everyone to gain experience. Without dark or gray entities on this planet, you would never have anything to bounce off. So we are convinced that they are part of the total scheme.

Why does someone like Ted Bundy, who looked all right, become a serial killer? You could have sat in a class with him, and he would have seemed like a nice, polite man. The soul chooses from the very beginning. Greed, jealousy, or avarice is the source of every wrong or evil. The dark entities cannot wait to come into life because they get riches, beauty, glamour, and everything else they want. Now that does not mean that everyone who attains beauty and glamour and riches is a dark entity—of course not! Some felt they would rather be top dog on the dark side than just a small light on the big side. What they did not realize was that in the larger picture, their light would have been brighter.

The dark are very perfected in their own way, because they became bad exactly as we became good. We have to stay away from them, but we learn from the evil they do. Have you not heard the expression, "But for the grace of God, there go I"? You can say you are hungry, but what do you want to eat? That's the way life is.

Do dark entities fear losing their identity?

No, neither grays nor darks give it any thought. A white always feels that way because, you see, a white entity has fought legions of dark to become its own individual part of God. That in itself is a glorious thing to stand, as Sylvia says, with your white plume and all your individuality intact and say, "I am the first captain of the first army; my name is so-and-so, and I am a warrior for God." Dark does not care—they walk around in cowls, all looking alike. They shuffle; they are dank and do not care.

Are there also "dark angels"?

No. We do not ever see dark angels. The dark Other Side is in a separate dimension and entirely on a lower, much more sluggish vibration. We see you very well, but we can barely see them. That's why it is so hard sometimes for us to protect you from them, because their vibration is so sluggish that we cannot even see them. We begin to watch you very carefully and see if you are reacting in a way in which you might be attacked, and then we start up our protection. That is why, sometimes, you get so mad at us and say, "Why didn't you get here sooner? Why have I had to go through this depression, this trial, this anxiety?" It is because we cannot see them very well.

Do dark entities have spirit guides?

No, they are just a conglomerate group. They do not have guides as you do; it is just a whole group of them that wander around. You have an individual guide with a name, a purpose, and a status. They do not. They are just an all-blended group. Do not misuse the word *guide*. They have no guidance. A guide says, "Watch out. Do this." They have nothing like that. They will stand around as observant sentinel figures. "Psychic thugs" is the best phrase for it.

Dark entities really do not have spirit guides as we know them. They will have reciprocation from the dark Other Side, but they do not have spirit guides like you have. They do not have a specially

assigned soul who wants to protect them. A dark entity is a very nebulous type. They are down here for destructive purposes, and that is
all. A trained assassin does not need any guidance. So they do not
have divine reciprocation.

They cannot really hurt you. That is why it is so ridiculous to think
that any dark entity can physically hurt you. You can only be psychically attacked in your emotions. Things can upset you or bother you,
but you cannot be physically hurt. Psychic attack is one of the main
reasons for a lot of illness and depression. I do not mean deaths, possession, or anything like that, but it is certainly a part of the depression and the anxiety that goes on with humankind.

How about gray entities—do they have spirit guides?

Yes, they do. If the entity turns black, however, the guide immediately recedes. I have never been a guide to a gray entity, but I do
know some who talk extensively with me about that. I have even
merged with them to get their feelings on this. It is so desperate. A
spirit guide can try to take a gray entity and turn them white, but the
minute they turn dark, the guide leaves.

A gray is allowed to select their guide. Dark entities do not stay
on the Other Side. They are pushed immediately into life. Those and
suicides come right back in.

Do grays still get guidance on the Other Side?

Yes. There is counseling. A gray entity can turn white, although
the greatest percentage of them do not. However, a dark entity can
never turn white. All of you have had counseling as well. In fact,
much counseling went on, as if you were training for a race: "Please
be careful of this, and especially that." But even with counseling, we
still know that when we come to this planet, all bets are off. Getting
from Utah to Vancouver can be achieved by many different paths, but
you will still arrive in Vancouver.

Does the Council allow the "desert" periods?

Yes, they allow these tests to occur. It is part of coming down to this plane. It is almost like generals getting together. Please do not misinterpret this statement—it is not that our Council hobnobs with the dark. No! But they are privy to what is going on with the dark. As long as you are on this Earth plane, you are subject to dark rule, unfortunately. Then the white spins into action to protect you. Once you are out on the battlefield, all we can do is try to run interference for you.

The minute you come down the chute, you have already "loosed the dogs of war." Every baby, we have said, should be born with a helmet and a gun, because that is exactly what they are doing—battling! The Council is aware of those times that are the most heinous for people. In doing that, they try to whip their own forces into action. The minute you come into life, you are pretty much in the dark.

Will there always be dark entities?

Always, for as long as anyone incarnates. When that schematic is ended, centuries and centuries from the present time, there will be no use for dark entities. I am sure that such knowledge is only within the mind of God about how much God wants to perfect His entities. Every time we ask, we are told that there are eons of time left. There are so many entities left to evolve.

The process of perfecting is like making a sword. You are tempered by fire just like the steel. If that steel had any consciousness, imagine its screaming. It has been burned and hammered, and yet what comes out is a perfect, beautiful sword. Yes, it takes a lot of burning and a lot of hammering to make your soul perfect.

How can we cope in these chaotic times?

Make sure you keep in touch with your own spirituality by being a part of some group. Without some inner golden thread, you can never feel totally comfortable. That is why eventually everybody will get into community living. It must be that way. To strengthen your spirituality on your own, you can certainly use the visualizations (discussed in Part III), such as mirrors pointing outward and the light of the Holy Spirit around you.

Set aside time to meditate, pray for each other, love each other, and give to each other.

The Eighth Level—Becoming Aware of Your Identity

If you have ever run across a person who is only on their third or fourth life, they are like babies. We've all been there: "It's a big, wonderful world, and I don't know who I am, where I am going, or where I have been." After that phase, the eighth level begins.

You know how at a certain age, maybe in your teens, all of a sudden you realized your identity. You began to definitively recognize yourself. That is what happens at level eight. You see that you are an entity who experiences suffering and pain. You begin to define yourself—your likes and dislikes, loves and hates, attributes and failings, what you care about. It is very much like realizing, "I have been here enough, and now I'm moving on."

Sylvia: This level is about realizing your identity and that you are made up of intellect and emotion. The only true identification lies not in social behavior: It is not who you are married to, which children you have raised, or where you live or work. This is not your true identity. The only identification that you ever truly have is that you are a direct part of God's intellect, here experiencing through the Mother God facet, Azna, our dear Blessed Mother.

That is the identity that you must know, because everything in life passes away, but not the love that we have for each other. That is the only one sustaining thing that we have. This building can go; the chairs, your home, your car, all these things get old. How you identify yourself is only by the love that you have of God and knowing why you are here and your love for each other. Each and every one of you are God. You must be. That is the identification. The same as our sons or daughters are products of us—we are the product of God. That is the greatest identity we can have.

These names, these faces, these bodies that we carry into life are nice sometimes. But this physical body is only rented. I want to know, though, when I was choosing my body, what was I thinking? I must have been busy talking and socializing and said, "I'll take something sturdy. Just put it over there, and I'll jump into it." But the marvelous thing about it is that in each lifetime, you are wool-gathering. You keep gathering all kinds of experiences and knowledge—and it is not from books. Certainly books will add to and validate your experience and knowledge, but where you really pull from, totally, is from your inner reaction and your viewing and experiencing life. That is where it comes from. All that information, once garnered, goes with you from life to life and continues with you on the Other Side. That is what makes it so wonderful. That becomes the identification of yourself experiencing for God.

The Ninth Level—a Fork in the Road

Francine: The ninth level is very important and definitive, because at that point, after you have lived several lives—usually it is about five—you decide, right then, whether you are going to take on more, or stop. I only took on one life on this planet. I have had many, surely, on other planets, but I was not stupid enough to come down here more than once. But I *was* stupid enough to take on being a communicating guide, a difficult job.

This is the time in which you became very definitive. It is almost what we call the second choice. "Do you want to stop, or go on and perfect further?" Truly, even though I am being a little lighthearted, most white entities raise their hands to go on to the ninth. At this level, you have had several lives—good, bad, or indifferent—but you want to perfect more for God. Numerology has a very ancient belief in the number nine, which is considered to be very high-blown, high-flown spirituality. The reason the nine is so ingrained as a highly spiritual number is that the soul actually picks, then, on the ninth phase, to go on further for its own spirituality.

The ninth level is almost a bail-out or exit level. Do you want to go further? There is certainly no stigma to exiting. Many have said, "That's it. I don't want any more." Some entities will stop on five—or even two or three—on one planet, but choose to go on and finish the rest on another planet. People are very territorial and usually become accustomed to a planet, bad or good, so they keep incarnating to perfect on that one planet. They can become almost victimized in their attachment to something. You certainly cannot blame people for staying here because it might take you 120 lives on another planet to do what would take you only three here. So it is more common to go through a few very hard lives than to take on 120 very benign ones.

Sylvia: Now, even without being psychic, we all know souls who are on a first, second, or third life. This is not a judgment. They sort of walk around wearing beanies with propellers. They just are not fully there, God love them. You can say, "My dog died, and my mother has cancer," and they go, "Okay." But that is not a judgment thing. The more lives you have, the more you love, the deeper your pain becomes. It is almost like pounding a fence post into the ground: The deeper it goes, the stronger it will be. You do not want a shallow one.

The higher the level of pain—the higher your level of loving and experiencing—the stronger that fencepost holds. If you were to drop food coloring in a pitcher of water, with one drop of red it gets a slight pink. But the more drops you add, the deeper it becomes. So each lifetime is a drop in that water that turns it emerald green or purple or whatever. Now there is nothing wrong with having a few lives. Francine only had one life on Earth. She said you can either incarnate here or work through your perfection by being a spirit guide. I imagine that, in retrospect, she would have rather lived many lives than be *my* spirit guide! I am sure it would have been easier. I asked her once if she ever wanted to be anybody's spirit guide again, and she said, "No." That gives you a good indication.

The Tenth Level—Choosing How Much to Open

Francine: How much knowledge do you want to acquire? This level is just as powerful as the previous one. You literally choose whether to open up all the way or only partially. Will you experience down to your very toenails or just a little bit? I am giving you a way to very definitively describe two types of people: With some, you wonder if they feel anything at all, but there are others who you know feel things head-on.

I think the reason we make such a fuss about the lifetimes here is because they are so laborious. Are they prideful? I think in the noblest sense of the word, they are prideful. Anyone who has ever had a lot of lives on this planet can be very proud of themselves for having sustained.

Sylvia: Now, the tenth level is very interesting. How much knowledge do you want to acquire? I know this is true in my heart; I think I have lived long enough to see it—some people really go out and live life on full tilt. Sure you get knocked down; you get smashed up a little bit, but wouldn't you rather know, at the end of the trail, that you lived it all and saw it all? The other extreme would be very much like if I said, "All right. We are all going to Egypt, and we'll all just stay in the hotel room. Or we'll only eat at Burger King." I did take a group to Egypt, and I had people on the trip who did that.

I felt like saying, "I took you all the way across these continents, and now all you're going to do is stay in your hotel room?" That is what some people do in life. They come into their body but stay in their hotel room. They do not go out and experience. They say, "Oh, but I am scared! What if I change jobs and move here and it doesn't work? What if I can't make it in this marriage? What if I get this car and it doesn't work?" So what! Unless you take chances, you experience nothing. So what if the car you get doesn't work? Then you get the experience of the fact that it didn't work. Maybe in the course of its not working, it stopped somewhere and you met a marvelous friend. Maybe the restaurant that you planned to go to one night was closed, and you went to some other little dive where you met somebody else who gave you something.

With experience, knowledge is acquired. If only we could look at life as a training, instead of acting like moths constantly flailing against a light, because when you get like that you just crash and burn. Why not circulate around the light? Even if you did hit the light, at least you would have done something rather than flap so far away from it that you never knew what it was like. The old expression is so true: "Better to have loved and lost than never to have loved at all." Of course, when you've just lost someone or something dear to you, you say, "I'd rather have not loved anything than go through this." But those lessons are the most significant ones.

If you always try to protect yourself from disappointment, you always have those bumpers on. We do, don't we? We shield ourselves. We put on weight, we put on masks every morning. It's all right. Sometimes we have to do that, but sometimes we have to be vulnerable enough to go down to the very bottom and then come back up— you have got to experience it. Try it! Go on a tram ride where you are dangling from a high wire. Try something! People say, "I don't know. I've never done that before." That's the *best* excuse to do it. Now, I don't mean we are all going to go skydiving today, but I think if that is what you want to do, that is what you should do. People say, "But what if I die?" That is the one thing we are *all* going to do. You see, I really am a predestinationist in this.

If you're going to die, you will. We could be sitting in a room, and the whole roof could cave in. When you are going to go, it doesn't matter where you are. But at the end of the trail, to be able to lie on your death bed, literally, and say, "I did it all! I grabbed every ring I could." That is the knowledge that I came in for. That is how the soul begins to expand. You know the Catholic prayer with the line, "My soul doth magnify the Lord!" How do you think your soul gets larger? How do you think your cup runneth over? Only if you experience! And don't gripe about it. There is nothing worse than walking down the street with people who are whining, "I don't want to do that. I don't like that." They are just a nightmare, aren't they?

If we have many lives, does it mean we are slow to learn?

Francine: That is the hardest thing to answer because some people want to experience more. That does not mean that anyone is better or worse, faster or slower. I think a better word would be more *curious*. Many tremendously evolved souls have had only three lives, and just as many very evolved souls have had more than 60 lives. Very unevolved souls could have 72 lives, or only 4.

I think people feel almost embarrassed anymore to say that they have had a lot of lives, for fear that somebody is going to think them either "overly spiritual or overly dumb," as Sylvia says. You will find that more curious souls will have more lives. That does not mean they are more advanced.

Now, the tenth level means that you have decided whether to be totally open or not. There is no discrimination either way. Many of you, like Sylvia, for instance, decided as a child to be very open, then got smashed up from life and decided to close off. I do not mean that you became cold, but the input was too great. You had a mission to perfect but realized that you came in too open and needed a trench coat to shield your vulnerability.

We are seeing so many people in this world getting to a point in which they have done all the wonderful, technical, great things they were supposed to do. Whether they were lawyers, merchants, or tailors, at some point they became terribly burned out. The reason they got so burned out is because they are at such a high perfection level—the tenth level—and they realized they were too open and needed to close off. However, this could be averted by getting to a place of spirituality, wherever that may be for you.

There is nothing worse than opening up to a spiritual belief and then being told that you are damned or bad. That makes your soul feel so shriveled. That's what religion did to you. It brought you in, gave you euphoria, and then damned you for your sin. That is a terrible cultural shock for the soul. You see, the soul comes in basically good, clean, trusting, gullible, emotional, loving, caring, and thinking. That is the way all souls were made. Life bludgeons the soul!

The Eleventh Level—Going Home

Sylvia: The eleventh level marks the end of the cycle of human lives as we know it. We go Home; this is the time to find your way back to the Other Side. Going Home! Isn't that a wonderful thing? You know the feeling: Every once in a while we meet someone and feel a connection. We meet a soul, outwardly like any other, and get a feeling that this one has wound its way to find us. You know there was a preordained reason that you were to come together for that brief moment, or for whatever time you are together, and we have a sense that we are Home. That is what going Home feels like—that fleeting euphoria, as if we could go forth and conquer the world. Nothing is going to be as bad as what we have already faced and gotten through. We can still love God through it all and be warriors for God. We will spend our time down here, see the sights, then go Home.

Francine: Your main job is to turn gray entities to white, with your love and unconditional giving, and it does not matter if what you give does not come back.. You often make it so difficult because you worry about where you are to work, who you are to marry, who you are to have as children, where you are to die and live—but your main job is just to love.

Can we fight the dark with righteous anger?

Oh, yes. That type of anger is good! Sometimes it's the only thing that works. Sometimes an emotion such as justifiable, righteous anger is the only thing. You must match emotion with emotion.

Please stop being so shy about venting your anger, tears, and frustration. Literally, for God's sake, be yourself. Let the tears and anger come out! It is inhuman to expect that of people—to be a submissive, sycophantic type of person. To stand and let someone defame or deface you is not what true spirituality is. No! You must come right back at those people—your family, friends, or anyone else. You have got to stop it right there!

I have always told you to be a soldier for God, even militant to a point. Now, you will not go around lopping off people's heads, but why should you dishonor yourself by putting up with somebody defacing your spirituality and your soul? That is an affront to the God inside you. If somebody approaches your altar, which is part of God, and talks to you disrespectfully, then you have every right to stand up and defend yourself.

Just today, we went to a lecture about how guides should constantly be trying to give people a better opinion of themselves so that they stand up and fight rather than cave in. Many religions want everyone to be mild and meek—to never question, stand up, or fight. What did they get? They got a herd of sheep! That advice bred ignorance, which promotes every kind of hellish manifestation. I am going to tell you something: Whenever a group is constantly fighting the devil, then the devil is alive and well right in the midst of them, because they will actually, literally create it.

The 12th Level—Resuming Life on the Other Side

The 12th level, of course, is returning to your original planet. Now everyone has a different status; your soul is at a certain level of development. Not only is this activated outwardly, but it is also intrinsically part of you.

No white entity could ever stand to lose themselves and become undefined. The 12th level, going back to your ultimate Home, hones your soul. It becomes sharper, with clear-cut edges. Notice, as you go through your last life, how definitive you become about your likes and dislikes, your loves and hates—you become sharply focused on things. That is the very definite mark of the 12th level and the final stage of your perfection. Really, the truest form of perfection is that you become fully defined. When this occurs, then you have finally found the unique particle of God that is indigenous to you.

Sylvia: The 12th level is finding your original home world to pursue higher learning, doing research, and knowing your unique God-

Center. Is it not wonderful to know that when we get to the Other Side, we are not going to be on a cloud with a harp? I know you will not believe this, but when I was a young girl, I used to challenge the nuns and priests all the time. When I was in the Episcopalian church, I used to challenge the bishop all the time. In Judaism, I challenged the rabbis. I was not exactly an obedient kid. This whole idea of going Home to the Other Side and continuing to work, I think, is the most marvelous thing.

We've all heard this: "You will go to the pearly gates and meet St. Peter. The streets will be paved with gold." If you came from a more Eastern philosophy, you are supposed to become part of the "amoebic cosmic" nebulous form of God. Or you might stand before the "Beatific Vision"—I used to just have a fit about that. I used to think, "If I'm not bored, God would be." Think!

Most religions believe in the survival of the soul. So why do some religious people deny the existence of ghosts? That is crazy!

Now, on the Other Side, what is so interesting is the amazing variety of activities possible. In orientation, we can help in- and outgoing souls; we have art classes, museums, and real work situations; we can have homes and our animals, but we do not have pollution; we do not have to have cars because we can *think* ourselves anywhere we wish to be; and we are with all our loved ones and wonderful animals.

Knowledge aids us along the path to enlightenment. You know what enlightenment meant to Siddhartha Gautama, the Buddha? Knowledge! It did not mean sitting cross-legged in a corner and chanting. It meant that you read, studied, learned, thought, and reasoned. You did not just accept somebody's word for something. You said, "Let me search and find out." Seek! In Luke 11:9, our Lord said, "Seek and ye shall find. Knock and it shall be opened unto you!"

The American Indians used to think the worst thing that could happen to a human being was to be ignored. If you are in a life situation in which you are being ignored, then for God's sake—the God within you as well as the God without—get out of it! You do not want to be ignored. I don't care if you have to wear a flag or a beanie with a propeller, but be of notice! Let the things that other people do fall away from you. Let the old hurts and barbs leave. Forget about them.

Put that garbage in a big trash bag and throw it away from you, because you do not want to carry that stuff with you to the Other Side. We want to be fresh and clean and be about our work. We want to hit the Other Side and say, "Here I am, and I feel great!" Francine said they are seeing souls come in now that are almost doubled over with pain, who must be cocooned and put to sleep for a while. I do not want to do that. I want to go over and hit the deck running.

"You are going to graduate from Life, whether you like it or not!"

— Sylvia

$ Chapter 9 $

SOULMATES

Francine: Most people need someone in their life, because that is the way you are made. As Sylvia says, "You were made with hands to hold, mouths to kiss, eyes to look through, and a body that fits into another one—whichever way you want to fit it." When you realize that you are pure energy forces, then every morning you should dress yourself as a pure energy force made by God, sent by God, and imbued with the best aspects of Mother and Father God.

Some of you have more feminine principle in you, or more male. Some have more yin than yang. There is nothing wrong with such a balance. If you are possibly too feminine in this life, it is because you have been too masculine in another, or because you are a female entity in a male body. On the Other Side, you were created as basically male or female. You might have wanted to take the chance of coming into a male body as a feminine entity just to experience what it was like, or vice versa. Very often such an entity will become gay or lesbian in that lifetime.

However, no matter whom you are partnered with on Earth, you must be constantly watchful and wary about what kind of energy is coming into you and what kind of energy the people around you put out. You must meditate upon this, and make yourself like a funnel or a sieve through which this negative energy flows away from you. You may say, "But if I realize the person I am living with is where the negative energy comes from, what should I do?" Then you must remove yourself from that person! It may seem heartless, but the one voyage you are on is that you are supposed to protect yourself on this island of thorns and happiness, of many sunrises and sunsets.

Begin to notice how you feel in the presence of certain people. Begin to notice how a daughter, son, husband, mate, spouse, or lover affects you. How good do you feel? You may say, "I don't feel bad, but I feel pity." Pity is a negative emotion! Sympathy, strangely enough, is not a negative emotion; rather, it means one soul feeling for another. But pity is more bone-deep than that—often it is created by the other party and put upon you. This is what we call "emotional blackmail."

Such people are being nothing but lazy! They are subconsciously thinking, *I want you to make me happy. If you don't, it's your fault.* As human beings, we are sympathetic in life, so we take this on. It becomes very flattering.

Twin Souls

Each person, as a created force, is duality—both male and female. Each pair of us, from the very inception of time, was made as a set of twin souls. There is another half of you. Everything in nature is imprinted and constantly repeated: the chain of love, the chain of power, the chain of male and female. God the Father is male, and God the Mother is female; and their creations continue this duality. Think of it almost as if it were a cut-out paper doll strung together; it is imprint upon imprint.

I want to get into some deep theological precepts about the twin soul—what everyone refers to, in your vernacular, as the *soulmate.* This term has been erroneously used. People in physical life constantly look for their soulmate; they become despondent if they realize that they are not with that entity. The Earth planet, unlike others, is not conducive to both souls coming down. The reason for this is that if one part of the twin soul is scarred too badly, the other part is also scarred. That doesn't help anyone, so the soulmate usually stays on the Other Side to guard, love, and guide the person, and be a partner to the spirit guide.

The soulmate does not guide and nudge as the spirit guide does, but gives their partner a "warming effect." It is the brief feeling that you sometimes get when you are alone—a sense of euphoria, a communion with yourself that is the other side of God's self coming toward you. Many people interpret this as a visitation of God, and of course it is.

The soulmate carries the best of you—a more complete you. It is like having a precious jewel that you entrust to a friend while you have to go into battle. If you are fearful of having certain parts of your soul damaged too badly, you leave them with your twin soul, who will carry them. If your sensitivity is excessive, you will leave some of it with the soulmate. If your ego could be bruised too easily, you will leave that. There have been soulmates that have come down together, but it becomes very difficult because there is such an empathy bond. When one is in pain, the other will manifest it, literally.

A *kindred soul* is one that comes down with you who is of the same mind-set. There is no doubt that souls advancing to higher levels—which you all are doing—will band together, and not have much in common sometimes with others. This is not due to "elitist" feelings or being arrogant; it is merely the same reason that seniors in high school do not run around with kindergartners. This is not to say that kindergartners are not wondrous, but in life you find people with whom you feel more of an affinity.

Every soul that comes down will, if they are smart, select a group of kindred spirits to come with them. When these magnets come together, then there is an instant affinity. One should marry a kindred spirit. One's best friend is a kindred spirit. The only problem is, the emotional hole left by the soulmate is very disruptive. It can lead to overt sexual behavior, which is an attempt to regain the missing love. But the force of sexual yearning sometimes disrupts the soul's total focus. A kindred soul is the friend who loves you for the total summation of whatever you will do, whatever you are, and whatever you are becoming, with no qualifications.

Let me explain how we were "conceived." I will use that word, since it is hard for the finite mind to realize that we always were, but we were not always in a state of singularity. Eons of time back, more time than any entity I know can truly remember, we were each part of an Uncreated Mass, but we still existed in mini-circles of light that were indigenous to our own souls. When we were spewed forth, as it were, we were made in dualities. We were made almost as a sort of monolith with a male and female facing each other. These dualities are as old as time: yin and yang, male and female, emotion and intellect.

Every dual entity was more or less "tubed" down and literally peeled from each other. Of course it had to be that way, because the male and female genetic strains had to be made as twin souls to manifest the Mother and Father sides of God. Not only is each soulmate pair divided so that one is male and the other female, but also within each individual resides both male and female qualities.

Is there a spiritual DNA?

Yes. It includes your theme, option line, dharma, karma, your experiencing, and your personality. Different facets. You have had the same temperament in every life. Sylvia has always had the same sense of humor on the Other Side in every life. It may be modified by life, but your likes and dislikes have been pretty much the same. Your tolerance level and your spirituality have grown, but the sum total of what you are has stayed individualistically you! We all keep our edges, which is wonderful, because that makes us individually different. That is the way God wants it. We all experience through our own spiritual DNA and feed that data back to God.

Are twin souls complete replicas?

They are complements of each other, and each part is complete. One is practical and the other romantic, or one is extroverted and the other more introverted. Together, they become dynamite. This is why it is not advantageous to have the soulmate incarnate with you—it is too similar in hurt and pain. Do not ever feel that a kindred soul cannot create this. A kindred soul, of the highest order, may have tracked through many lifetimes with you and played many parts with you in this play of life. The human soul has this yearning to find the other side of itself. This is the one driving force that gets souls through life. It is the carrot in front of the donkey's nose.

Can a person have no soulmate?

The male counterpart of the female soulmate must *earn* her. I know this may sound funny since they came together, but the minute you become incarnate, everything must be earned.

The male, through his lifetimes, petitions again for the other side of himself. Why does the male do it rather than the female? That is just the way it's set up. Then at the final hurrah, as you might say, when all lives have been lived, the soulmates come together, which is in itself an exultation. Now you may wonder, if you had each other once, and you split apart, why do you have to earn them back? It is because both halves must be at an equal level of evolvement to be reunited.

There are some entities, too few to number, who choose not to go back and cement again with a soulmate. Now that shows you, beyond any shadow of a doubt, the true definitiveness of the personalities. Even on the Other Side, people still have their differences. Of course, they still love each other, but they do not choose to be in or have the closeness that they once had. So they do become very individualistic. Sometimes life's experiences create such differences that a person outgrows even their soulmate. There have been rare cases in which soulmates trade. It is just that another entity fits better or that a kindred soul becomes far more important to the entity than the soulmate ever could be.

The soulmate situation is grossly overrated; it simply means that some people decide to go back to the one with whom they were created. But in the travels of life, sometimes souls will choose to be with someone else. Not often, but sometimes souls will find that as they evolve, even in one lifetime, they will outgrow others. Let us say that John Doe picks a very harsh reality, and Jane Doe, his soulmate, picks a very frivolous one. At the end of, let's say, 15 lives, do you think that John will have the same feelings or preferences that she has?

So now you are in life and have begun to garner knowledge. As you do so, you begin to assimilate more; your soul begins to grow and "magnify the Lord," as Sylvia loves to say. As it does, you may find that your soulmate is no longer up to your level. That does not mean that the soulmate does not stay over on the Other Side, watching out for you, loving you, and staying a friend. Of course they will remain so and be close. That, too, is part of an entity's homesickness—they miss the Other Side, but they also miss the other part of themselves.

It is very rare and almost never happens that one's soulmate is incarnated in this life. People are constantly asking, "Where is my soulmate?" It is perfectly correct to answer, "On the Other Side." The chance is one-millionth of one percent—even that is high—that the soulmate ever incarnates, unless there is a specific, horrendous mission, and then the soulmate may come down to help. But because the soulmate is so like you, usually it is not functional. It is like having another "you" walking around. Psychologically, that becomes a borderline situation.

Males can petition to have a certain person as their soulmate. It sounds almost like a betrothal. Sometimes, as you well know, in the soul's evolvement, an entity may turn away from the light, as with a gray entity. One turns black and the other one stays gray or turns white. What would a person do in that case? There must be multiple choices of whom the person ends up with, and love that transcends all. People feel that because you are made with somebody, you have to stay with that person. That is wrong! In the travels of life, you may find someone who is far more companionable or who loves you very much.

In planning a life, many can stand in line for one group of parents, or a particular parent they want. In fact, if they do not get into line right away, they may have to choose another vehicle. However, the replacement must fit the same program, or very close—the same geographical area or the same cultural group. There are many variables. But most of the time, the entities will stand in a group, choose who they want, and then write their charts, almost like you would write a play or a script.

Most of you, being Gnostics, did not pay particular attention to the genes you were choosing. In other words, you knew your mission was to get down, so you took the first available train. I am sure most of you must realize that, because you have got to be sitting there wondering why in heaven's name you picked some of the parents and things that you did! You had to get in, so instead of taking a luxury liner, you came by freighter or any vehicle available.

Marry and partner with someone whom you love, who is a friend, who respects you, and who loves you *for you*. Quit looking for a fluttering heartbeat, stars in the sky, and bells ringing in your ears. That is nothing but a hormonal flux. It was only put there for childbearing! Look for the truest form of kindred soul.

Are twins the same soul?

No. They are born with separate souls, but they are genetically linked by their cellular structure. There is nothing more humbling in the world than twins: You have an exact reflection of yourself and can never be unique in this world.

Why would one soulmate evolve more slowly than the other?

They did not pick as many different, varied experiences as their partner, or maybe one mate did not learn as quickly as the other. You could have a soulmate on the Other Side who is very elevated and you are just babyfied, for example. There is no such thing as a male entity coming over completely unconnected to a female entity. I know of only one male entity who chose not to. He chose to go off and be alone, but they are still connected by the fact that they were created together. We get the idea, because we are so finite, that soulmates go back and make this wonderful union, sticking together exclusively to do everything and running around as a closed group. No! That is not the way it is. It was only set up that way for the creative process.

Do soulmates travel through universe after universe together?

Yes, many times. There is a bond there that can never be severed. The love bond between that male and female is something that continues, but you might not want to spend eternity with this one person. The idea that we all go over and just hole up with our soulmate is wrong. I have a wonderful soulmate by the name of David; I see him very rarely and I love him very dearly. But I certainly would not want to feel that my whole evolvement was based on whether I was going to go back and cleave only to him.

Most of the time when you are in life, the soulmate is on the Other Side. In a sleep state or a waking one, you can ask for your soulmate to come and help you. The soulmate can occupy an astral state and be in both places at once. In other words, you can astrally project yourself to your soulmate, or they can be omnipresent in life, or they can be present with you in spirit form. They have visiting rights.

⚬ ⚬ ⚬

"It is in loving that you expand your soul.
God's truth is so simple. It is so beautiful.
It is that God loves you, and you love God."

— Francine

Chapter 10

Physical Universe

Francine: Earth is the most difficult of all planets. I can only tell you this before God, and this is the Gospel truth: There is no planet in all the galaxies any harder than this planet that you call Earth. It has every adversity. It is known throughout the whole universe as the Dark Planet of Insanity. This is the primary home of many dark entities. In the philosophy of Novus Spiritus, you were always told that there is a "dark" planet. What you were not told was that you are on it! I can truthfully tell you from all my research and what I have observed that there are none as bad as this one. There are battles fought elsewhere, but not like on this planet!

Earth seems to be the cesspool for all negativity throughout the universe; it has all ended up in this waste dump! So when you strong-hearted souls decided to come down, you really picked the harshest level to come into. If for no other reason, you should be very proud of yourself for having decided to take the chute down even once.

This is a planet in which, when you come down, even though you have charted your life, anything can be "up for grabs," as you say in your slang. This planet is so hard to chart for people because the minute you come into this planet, you go into a very dark labyrinth. That is why you pull in extra guides. That is why we try desperately to attend to you more. Your soul yearns for not only the Other Side, but also for the bodily memory of places that only exist on Earth. It is very much like knowing you must go through surgery and knowing that it is painful, and then having it done and wishing you could take it back, but you cannot. You have already gone under the knife, and all you can do is endure it until it heals.

I do not want to paint a black, negative picture. What I want to do is inform you of how brave you are to have come here, and how much you are growing spiritually! On the Other Side, you are approaching the highest plane that you can possibly choose. There are billions of entities who would never come here no matter how much counsel they received. Those of you who are spiritual warriors have come here and have faced all adversity.

I don't like this expression: "God only tests those who can take it." That sounds as if God is playing a game with your soul. That is not true, although there is truth in saying that through adversity, you do learn. If you had no challenges, would you be as strong as you are today? You would not have been able to test your mettle. However, that is not the reason adversity is here. It was not created for that. It is just part and parcel of this Earth. The minute you set foot on this planet, it is going to happen. Certainly you choose a lot of it, just by being here. Even if you have not had a hard life, that doesn't mean that you are not an advanced soul. Just surviving this life and living here is enough!

Without hardships, the soul evolves less and more slowly. That is why this planet is marvelous in its own right, even though we talk about the horror and atrocities. But it is one of the fastest places to grow. From the adversity of this planet springs forth some of the greatest, most beautiful gems that we have in the whole universe. In great trials, when one's life has been tested beyond all measure, one survives and flourishes beyond that. To tell you the absolute truth before God, anyone who wants to evolve to any significant point must come to this godforsaken planet! It is one of the last testing grounds for survival against the dark. This is where "the final cut of the cloth is made," as they say.

Many entities will postpone coming to this planet for eons for fear that their soul is in jeopardy, especially the entities that are right on the fringe of gray. The white entities do not mind it so much, except they know they are going to be crucified. Yet once you emerge from such hardship, it is so glorious.

Other Life Forms

In Chapter 1, we talked about how the universe is shaped like a great man, with Pisces as the feet and Aries as the head. I myself tried to visit the farthest reaches of the great man—from head to foot—and in my travels, I have not found anything or anyone that is not of human quality. They all look like us. We do not see any extraterrestrials (ETs) as you have imagined them—no three-fingered salamanders or anything green; no funny skin. They may be shorter, lighter, or taller with large eyes, but you would certainly know that a Pygmy was human, would you not? The Watusi, even though they are seven or eight feet tall, are certainly human. Nothing in the universe has one gigantic, cyclops eye. Such ideas are the offshoot of your fear and ignorance.

We are really resentful of movies and books that scare everybody with images of these awful little gremlin things piercing people's brains. We do not know of any inner or outer galactic entity that does this. A humanoid is never to be mistaken for anything else. That is why we find it garishly funny. No one that we know of in the whole galactic universe looks like a monster. They might have bigger eyes, ears, or noses, but everyone looks like a human being or has humanoid qualities.

The constant recycling of entities, called reincarnation, has always been. In the scope of reincarnation, we also have to talk about colonization. Primitive tribes know this to be true. The colonization was made on this planet millions of years ago when these planetary entities were sent. The first set came as adults and failed miserably because of disease and the planet's terrain. Future groups succeeded.

Mission Life Entities

Almost all of you are on your last life. You will then go to the Other Side and decide where you want to go from there. If you do decide to take up a mission, you could be assigned to any galaxy.

Every tenth life, usually, you can rest assured you are again going to find yourself on a planet fighting against the dark. The amazing thing is that Jesus said in his writings that if you do not want to do it, then you should not take the first hop! You take that first "hop" to the Pleiades or any of the other millions that even the astrologers have not named.

When you separated from the Divine, some of you decided to become mission life entities, in which you took on missions for God that can span multiple lives. They will take you through nine other planetary systems living one life on each, then on the tenth system, you might have to spend 30, 40, or more lives, then fight the battle in the end. The reason that some choose to become mission life entities is to help other people and attain the Light of Gnosis, the light of sacred truth. This is very much what Jesus meant when he said, "Seek and ye shall find; knock and it shall be opened unto you." Most of you, because you are worn out and tired, say that you will not come back to this planet again, and you will not!

Can we take a vacation on another planet?

Oh, yes. Of course we do. We have to go someplace, the Pleiades or somewhere, to get some kind of breather. Other, less dark planets can really make entities feel that they have gone to heaven. They still have to work through toward perfection, but they don't have these dark, endless nightmares coming at them, testing them. The problem here is that darkness can invade your dreams and create nightmares.

Andromeda tests entities as well, but it is much more of an intellectual test. It is very much like the Other Side in that each person attains their goal through researching and working, and they compete with themselves rather than the egos of others.

Who colonized Earth initially?

Andromeda. They did Venus at the same time they did this plan-et. Venus, at that point, was in a different orbit and could sustain life. Both Mercury and Mars had life at one point. That is what the gullies, canals, and riverbeds of Mars are.

Now when Andromedans came, the adults died and could not even procreate. Some years later, they sent Asian-looking children. There were 32 children brought with two adults, a male and a female. Out of those, 24 children made it, and they intermarried. That is when the creative force started on Earth. The first colony that died was in Australia, which was too arid. Ethiopia, even though hot, still sus-tained life. It became like the movie *Lord of the Flies*—children ran wild on the planet, grew up, procreated, and then seemed to accli-mate. The Andromedans realized they had a new place where they could send their people.

This planet was very hard for some reason (I am told in records) to get to a point where human life could be sustained. It is very small, there is too much water, and it is unusable water to boot. The whole terrain is mostly unusable. You have far too many deserts. The configuration on the Other Side matches that of Earth, but the land mass is larger on my side. There are oceans, but you do not need that much water.

You may ask me, "What role does God play in all this? If this seems like such a physical phenomenon, then is God not omnipresent?" Of course. God not only set it into motion, but He keeps it rotating by His omnipotent presence. The Unmoved Mover is the principle by which everything moves—one static, constant, con-tinuous thing. If I set something into motion that goes on perpetual-ly, am I not still the One who set it into motion? My being, watching it, keeps the top constantly rotating. Absolutely!

Death Without Pain

Each planet has its own Other Side, and some of these are so much more advanced than Earth's. All are beautiful and have almost the same configuration, of course not with Earth's geographical features, but beautiful landscapes. The amazing thing about other planets is that when you get ready to leave your physical body, you just step through a cloud that appears. There is no such thing as death, except on this planet.

Can you imagine it? You live to be a certain age; you are very healthy and vibrant—then when your time comes, you have an instinctive calling, a cloud appears, and you step through it. We make such a big to-do about death in this life because the material world holds on so strongly, and you hold on to it so strongly.

How is romantic love different on other planets?

On Earth, you have a practice of pairing off in couples. On other planets there are conglomerate loves. That does not mean that it is a free-for-all of sexual promiscuity. I do not mean that. It just means that people are together in groups, very loving and merging. No one says, "This person is mine and not yours; don't you look at them." The other aspect, procreation, is also so much more beautiful because— and men are not going to like this—the choice of mate is made by the woman. She chooses based on genetics.

What is a black hole?

A black hole is nothing but a vacuum cleaner for the universe. It is a garbage collector. The universe has more mass than you think. It is very high-density mass.

What is the Bermuda Triangle?

There is a similar triangle in Java, and also in the state of Nebraska, strangely enough. They are holes in the space-time continuum into which time slips. They were purposely put there by God, and any intergalactic person knows that they are highways. Some extraterrestrials used them to get to this planet instead of taking spaceships. They seem to be the only ones who know how this works.

In the last few thousand years, you have lost your knowledge about teleportation. So what happens now is that people get into these highways and they cannot get out. It is a slippage. What is amazing about this is that it is a fairly complex navigation; they are more open and visible at certain times of the year, just as certain mountain roads may be closed at certain times of the year due to rain or snow.

There was a famous case in Nebraska where a man walked out of his house and slipped into one of these, and they could hear him screaming for three days in the atmosphere above them. They are nothing more than teleportation units, or highways, in which people could travel in and out of other planetary systems. You do not know how to use them.

How many people are allotted to Earth?

There were ten billion allotted to this planet. You only have about six billion incarnate now. If four more wanted to come in, you would have ten billion, but you could not support it. Other planets have 22 billion. It just depends on how many entities need to perfect, but they were all made identically at once and always were.

God, in His quest for experiencing and because of His complexity, had to have a trillion, billion, million. He had to know all the facets of every single, solitary nuance of emotion. Think of your own mind. How many synaptic references do you think you have? Would you not say that with your mind you've had millions? Now consider God's mind. There would have to be millions upon millions of those. Your own flare is unique and for God.

The big argument people have used against reincarnation is this: If there are no new entities, why is the Earth's population growing? That is so ridiculous. There are allotted to this planet alone over ten billion. There are only about six billion down now. That is not counting the entities coming through from Andromeda, Crab Nebula, and all the others.

In this dark planet, where the rules are much more stringent, you touch the heart of piety and spirituality. Once you embrace spirituality, you can never break that covenant with yourself. Once you make the choice—and it is a religious, spiritual quest, truly a Gnostic test—if you break that covenant, you make yourself pay dearly. No one else makes you pay. The covenant is between God and you to come down and bring enlightenment to the world, to get this terrible dark planet into light and free of guilt, horror, and the fear of devils and demons. What better place to do it than on the very ground in which dark entities roam. So you do have a battle!

This is the only planet in which disease exists. On all other planets, when one is ready to die, they cross the threshold and just go. They literally step out of their body, their body slumps, and they cross the line into the Other Side. This is the only planet in which people do not find their ultimate partner and stay with them. Procreation is not as great on other planets, but merging is. Procreation is so prevalent on this planet, of course, for a very spiritual reason. It is because all the entities that want to perfect quickly are going to rush in now and try to finish up all the hard lessons. This is why your population is exploding.

Those of you who are living out a life, think about all the people you have known who have completed their graduation faster than they could on any other planet. It takes bravery and stamina, but there is also a great and glorious plus to all this. If you wish, you may live fewer lives because you have completed so many spiritual tests that you never have to complete anywhere else. Every one of you who has taken on this spiritual mantle has been tested sorely. Everything has been dropped into your path like a crucifixion or a lion's den. These kinds of tests are not on any other planet.

Religion

Religion does not exist anywhere else but on this planet. Spirituality exists throughout the galaxies, but this is the only place in which *religionistic* practices seem to have taken hold. The term *religionistic* means that there is nothing but ritual, confinement, persecution, dogma, sins, and rights and wrongs. All of you who believe in the spiritual world are religious without being religionistic. *The Book of Life* is known throughout all the galaxies. It is known as a book of wisdom, and it is very beautiful, bound in white and gold, containing all the writings of all the Masters, not only here but in other places.

This planet does not take well to any avatar or person who wants to create good. Many of you must really be watchful of being a warrior entity. That does not mean you go around brandishing a sword. No matter what, you must keep your own spirituality clean. Do not let anyone frighten, demean, criticize, or hurt you. Not for your sexual preferences, your love of life, the way you have raised your children, or your choice not to have children—not for anything can you allow people to demean you. This is the only planet in which people demean others.

Of course you have dark entities around you. They do nothing but incarnate on dark planets. They never go to the Other Side. As soon as they are dead, they come right back into another body. So when they die, for them the tunnel goes from here directly to a fetus, then right out into the world again. So don't worry about ever meeting a dark entity on the Other Side. The only domain they have is an Earth life or another planet, although most of them are here.

How did racial diversity occur?

You were colonized from at least four planets. Let us take the Watusi tribe, for instance—they were colonized by a planet in Andromeda who sent their very tall and dark children. Another planet also sent smaller people, and thereby you have the Pygmies. Africa is the seat where it all started. In the beginning, the black race was dominant. At least three or four planets that I know of colonized in different places. That is what the Bible tried to explain with the Tower of Babel—everybody began to try to get higher and higher up, which really meant coming down here from upper worlds.

Different entities chose to use different visages. Other galaxies contain every race you could ever think of and even some that you have never seen. People become very attached to a certain visage and then begin to colonize in that visage. After the first colony, many colonizations of races and cultures came in from other galaxies as long as they knew that life would be sustained.

God created different races on other planets, and they all began to migrate here. For instance, the Zulus also come from a different planet. The only reason I am making such a to-do about Africa is because that it is where it all began. That is really, on my side, where Eden resides—the seat of the birth of humankind.

The Dogan tribe in Africa, beyond a shadow of a doubt, knows about Ceres and the Dog Star, yet there is no way to see either one from Earth without a gigantic telescope. The reason they know is that their heritage and their tradition tells about people coming from the Dog Star. Their tradition knows this to be true. Because they have been isolated from the outside world, their tradition has stayed clean, clear, and pure. Unlike the written word, many times the traditional word, even though it takes on gigantic flavorings, can stay more true—there are no monks sitting in little cells and embroidering the story any way they wish to, as was done with the Bible.

Do we have past-life recall from other planets?

Yes, but not as much, because this is the one planet in which phobias occur, and they are the main cause of morphic resonances. You are not going to have bleed-throughs from other planets because you do not have any phobias there. This dark planet is what causes phobias and fears. We do not know of anyone on other planets that has a fear of drowning, wide-open spaces, small spaces, or anything else. That is not known.

Where are UFOs from?

Most of these entities are visiting from Andromeda. Andromedans colonized Earth, and they keep coming back to see how their entities are doing. They are very sad about the whole thing, by the way, because of what has been done to this planet. I think what is really terribly unfair is that the Andromedan people have been portrayed as frightening. The only way anyone could be frightened is because it is out of their realm of knowledge. No one reading this would be frightened by being taken, because their spirituality would be high enough to know what these entities were doing.

The space suits they wear look a little bit different because they cannot endure this atmosphere. The large eyes that some have described are nothing but windows in a helmet. If you walked up to one of our spacemen, you would say, "They have glass for a face. They have no eyes, nose, or mouth." The atmosphere in which Andromedans live is so much lighter and less dense than Earth's.

Their eyes and nostrils are somewhat larger, but by no means would you feel they are not human. Many people have been visited and have wonderful feelings of bliss and love—they do not get traumatized at all!

What are the crop circles?

They are a map of the galaxy from whence they came. However, your astronomers are not smart enough to figure out where the galaxy is.

There has been so much activity as far as UFO sightings. You have been visited by both inter- and extraterrestrials. Do you know the difference? Extraterrestrials come in a human form from another planet. Interterrestrials are what I am, which means we are in spirit form. We are able to have direct communication with extraterrestrials. We do not have direct communication with you. This does not mean that they are more highly advanced, but just that they are less dense.

People on other planets have direct recourse from their spirit guides. They straddle both dimensions. They appear and disappear so quickly because they have learned dematerialization. They also, like in your TV show *Star Trek,* can be molecularly diffused and reassembled. They have a mechanism in which they can beam themselves to different places.

Recognizing Other Souls

I have only had one life. On the Other Side, I chose to look as I did in that one life because I had no other reference. However, I have been a guide on this side for such a long time, and I have learned so much more. You can change your visage, but the most marvelous thing is that your appearance does not matter. Souls recognize each other on any level, whether short, tall, thin, heavy, black, red, or whatever. For a long time, Sylvia walked around in an Asian visage because she just liked it; she had six Asian lives. Then she changed, but everybody walked up and said, "Hi." They knew who she was.

You will pick your visage from one or a combination of lives. Perhaps you liked the height of one, the figure of another, and the skin color of a third. You can pick and choose. When a soul returns to my side and a relative comes to meet them, that relative will take on the visage with which the entity knew them.

So many times you will ask of me, or another spirit guide, how one soul recognizes another. The answer is that the soul eyes recognize each other. It does not matter what visage is worn. An almost strobe-like effect is reflected on the physical retina of the eye, which recognizes the psychic qualities of another person. This is what causes so many of you to be approached with questions, because your aura shows it and your physical eyes reflect it.

On your side, you also recognize a soul immediately. You may not have the name, or an exact recollection of where you knew a person from, but you must have felt at times that you've known someone forever. That is soul recognition. On the other hand, you may meet others whom you feel you could never tolerate no matter what they did—that is also soul recognition. That person might have created a terrible situation for you in some life, and even though on my side the soul totally forgives, in life it is not that easy. It is very necessary to have some type of unforgiveness in order to stay in life. Not necessarily having vengeance, but being able to vent your anger toward a person is normal, even feeling that you want them dead. That is a human thing.

When you pass through the veil and come to the Other Side, then you can get into the more quiet, peaceful mode of forgiveness, and have total recognition. The more you advance spiritually, the more you are going to have soul recognition. Even more important, souls will have recognition of you. They will sense your feelings, your love, the innermost workings of your soul.

Your Appearance on the Other Side

I want to talk to you about your visage. In some lifetime, or at some point in creation, you have picked a visage that you find favorable. You may pick the looks of a Japanese girl, a Germanic person, a Hawaiian, a Jamaican, or whatever culture. Many times the visage is adopted from a life that you have particularly loved. If that is not acceptable, you can form your own looks.

I have kept my visage of an Aztec-Incan female. As you well know, I have only had one life. Now, who gave me the visage in the first place? I created it, and it just happened to coincide with the place in which I lived. The only problem I had is that I did create myself a little bit taller than most Aztec-Incan females were. You may say, "What about genetics?" It is true that we have to manipulate our genes, so if we want to have light hair and eyes, we would not necessarily pick an African couple for parents.

Our structural visage can be in any size, shape, or form. We have a sexual identity on the Other Side. We stay basically either male or female, whichever we originally chose to be. It seems to be about half and half. It is always human: No one comes over and immediately goes into becoming an animal. No entity has ever transmigrated. You do not start out as a beetle, then become a dog, then something else. No! Those other life forces are pure and totally unto themselves.

Now a very strange thing happens. If you have abused your body in life, then what we call the "flaw situation" occurs on my side: You are not allowed to be as attractive as you wish to be. A beautiful visage has to be earned, just like everything else. If you have had a life of tremendous overindulgence or debauchery, then you will not have a perfect visage. I do not mean just a glass of wine or overeating, but something really detrimental such as excessive use of alcohol, drugs, or something similarly mind-altering. When this occurs without rehabilitation in that lifetime, then when you come over, your visage will show it.

Also, everyone on my side has a flaw. I have a chip in my tooth. Sylvia has a crescent-shaped scar under her right eye, a small scar. Others may have a white streak through their hair, or some irregularity to show that we are still ascending toward perfection.

Total perfection does not mean we go back into the Uncreated Mass, but it means we are still experiencing for God, learning for ourselves, and also showing our imperfections. It has always been a reflective need and desire for all entities to physically show their imperfection. It is amazing to see a soul's defects dim as they advance. Many entities like to keep some of their defects because it lets them realize that they still have eternities to go through before they really, truly feel that they have reached their ultimate nirvana.

Quadrants

I think it is very interesting to know the physical geography of any place, so I want to talk to you about the meaning of the quadrants on the Other Side. The continents on my Side are in exactly the same place as Earth's. The formation of our land is exactly like yours. We are a mirrored image of you. We have all the oceans, islands, mountains, canyons, and everything identical to yours, except without the spoilage.

Everything is in the same configuration, but of course we run at a higher vibration with more intensely beautiful colors. We do not have pollution, freeways, or cities as such. We do not have any beer cans, smog, plastic, or anything like that. We do not have houses like eruptions all over the landscape. Our animals are not killed. Please realize that your world, Earth, is a shadow world. If you look very closely, you will see that your world is nothing but a faded image of what the Other Side really looks like. It is tragic in many ways; it is much like giving a child a piece of dollhouse furniture that is a perfect

Queen Anne replica, and they destroy it, but the original piece stands. Yours is a papier-maché world. This was only a synthetic place that was here to harbor you and make you feel less out of sync with your homeland.

On my Side, there are places in which we can reside. We like a more pastoral look. You must realize we do not sleep, eat, go to the bathroom, or any of those other maintenance things that humans must do. You will find this very convenient.

Each continent is divided into four sections. In certain parts there is just animal husbandry, for example, or orientation that goes on. It is very much like when you go to a mall to shop. We go to the quadrant of animals to see our animals, or to the quadrant that hosts the research center, or whatever. It is quite nice that way. Your experiences in life determine which quadrant you wish to work in.

These quadrants are secure because we do not allow any alien, dark entities in. Not that that would be a hazard, but it is a protection. We have never had an invasion of any kind, and the dark entities keep to their own Side so we are not apt to mingle. We are even very conscientious about gray entities that might get in.

Being able to *think* yourself to any place is wonderful. You do not have to walk if you don't want to. If you are in the quadrant for animal husbandry and you want to go elsewhere, you just think yourself there. You are immediately there.

We have a research quadrant, which sounds very formal but is not. There is another quadrant for artistic and musical endeavors. The quadrants are basically, I do not want to say roped off, but you know where you are supposed to go. It also helps us with incoming and outgoing souls. If you were to die on another continent, you would probably check back into the continent on which you had lived most of your lives. That is why some people elevate above their body while others go directly to the tunnel. The difference is that some people are traveling to get back to their quadrant.

It is all very systematic. It sounds almost cold, does it not? It is not. It has all been laid out with perfect wisdom and guidance. It is simplified, but more systematic and organized than your world will ever be. Our world is not chaotic, not filled with traffic, noise, and people running into each other. We have none of that. People have often asked me, "Do you eat?" We can if we wish, but nothing has much of a taste so we choose not to. The only time we ever use some fruits and things is when we are trying to mimic the congeniality and amiability of getting together, but we soon learn not to.

Sylvia always says she is going to eat a thousand chili cheese dogs when she comes over, but they will not have any taste. We find that souls who have just recently come in, souls newly arrived, have a tendency to want to eat when they come over, but soon tire of it.

We saw a man come in the other day who wanted a turkey sandwich. Some of us had forgotten how to even think "turkey"—on the Other Side, "thoughts are things," so to help him, they tried to create a turkey sandwich.

The Physics of the Other Side

We on the Other Side are total matter; you are anti-matter. You are woven very loosely and poorly in molecular structure. We are denser, and what is more strange, our air is more rarefied. We are denser and of greater matter, yet millions of us could occupy a room in your world.

It is almost impossible to tell you the laws of our physics, because while you have three dimensions, we have far more. We have cubes within cubes, and dimensions within dimensions that we can see. We see your dimension, our dimension, and future dimensions. We have a creative force for dimensions.

Do we have walls that we can touch? Yes. We have temples in which we can reside and ground on which we walk. We also have sexual communion with each other, but it is quite different. If you wanted to share my essence, you would walk through me and I would walk through you. We can do that and still maintain our own substance. Now, the merging for a love affair takes longer. It is so advantageous to share the love of another without any of the moral issues that you face. There is no one running off with your spouse. There is no childbearing and all those other taboos that you have in life that are necessary to build your society. We are not bound by those.

Can we visit the Other Side?

Yes, through hypnotic regression. You then realize the whole pattern of why you are here. You realize how each little square adds up to a whole quilt, instead of just seeing one little square at a time. It is wonderful to visit past lifetimes, because then you fully understand your theme. But why not go to the Other Side, too? You then realize why you went through what you did. Sylvia has done thousands of regressions and has only found a few who wanted to go to the Other Side. Most of them just wanted to go to life after life after life, and nothing in between. Ridiculous!

The Relationship Between Spirit Guides and Us

In order for me to reach the sixth level, I had to commit to being a communicating guide. I was so amazed at the broadening of my mind by touching this level. A wonderful euphoria of knowledge poured in. I had access to unbelievable vistas of knowledge. I said, "I will do anything to achieve that level." Now that I've been a guide, I am not sorry for my choice, but I did not realize how hard it would be.

You must realize that in order to be a spirit guide, we need to become somewhat humanized. We are not like the Archetypes or other entities that come around, such as the protectors or the infusers of knowledge, although we can be. But as communicating guides, we must be on your level of feeling, which is very hard for us because we are then both finite and infinite, which creates a very hard schism. While we are guides to you, we cannot be with the groups that we would usually be with. All the guides stick together. We are not really allowed to be with the general population because we are very heavy. We are more earthbound, yet we have higher knowledge from the Other Side, and we have to take on the mantle of your heaviness. This is not to make you feel sorry for us—we will benefit from it. But that is why most entities do not choose to be a guide more than once.

Not everyone chooses to be on a high level. You may stay at any level you wish. I saw someone the other day trying to decide whether or not to go up a level on our Side, and it was too much. The person decided to stay put.

Your spirit guides are with you all the time—every minute. The ringing in your ears is often your spirit guide. They can hear you speak to them. They hear every whisper that you make. If you think you are frustrated, you should see your guides trying to get through the muck and mire to get to you. You could say the tiniest whisper, and they would hear it. If you give them consent to read your mind, they would hear your thoughts, too.

How do they feel when things go wrong for us?

It is terrible. It is our perfection scheme, too. I think people do not realize that while you are perfecting, so is your spirit guide. Your guide experiences what you do. The closer we are to you, the more we are the loved one for you. It is like watching your child go through something—you are screaming and yelling. I have actually witnessed guides screaming and jumping up and down trying to warn somebody.

When our loved ones suffer, we suffer, too, because we have become humanized. If I was not humanized to a point and you asked me about your dog or your family, I would simply say, "Well, they are going to die and come home." It would not matter. I would not be able to relate to you or understand your reactions.

Does our guide ever "burn out" and leave us?

No. Especially in hard times, I have seen guides lined up at the Council trying to petition for help for their loved one, as we call them. We do stand around and get very aggravated when things are hard.

I yell at the Council. I have even gone over their heads, as all guides will. Our democracy is very much like the Greek Senate. We can appeal to a higher power and get something done. After a period of counseling, then we can go behind the Godhead for advice from those who have merged there. If that does not work, we can go directly to Azna for an audience.

A lot of times, people will bring in extra guides if they are in dire straits and need help, when they are down, or if they have just asked for more spiritual infusion. An additional guide would be assigned to help your main guide. But usually there is just one communicating guide; any more would be a drain on your energy.

Through all our lives, have we had the same guide?

No. We could not take it! For example, Fletcher, the marvelous spirit guide who spoke through medium Arthur Ford, was so cute after Arthur died. He said he would never be a guide again, and he never has been. He has been so reclusive. We go and ask him for advice, but he does not even want to talk to us. He is so sick of it. I am not too sure I will not feel the same. Not because I do not love humanity, but just because it seems that people think guides are infallible and that they are not humanistic. They are! They are very humanistic, but lack a human form.

Does our guide experience what we go through?

Yes, it is a learning experience for both. You see, there is never a time when we stop perfecting. I think people believe that to guide someone, you must be perfect. It is true that our knowledge is far greater than yours because you are in a dense atmosphere and cannot see the whole picture. But by far, we are not the ultimate source of knowledge. We are mentors, helpers, and protectors, but we do not have supreme knowledge.

How do we get our guide?

I petitioned the Council for Sylvia, just as your guides petitioned for you. You meet each other and make an agreement or contract between you. You also have a period of time in which you train. You select your guide, and she or he selects you. Many times we are in the state of bilocation. We can be with you and somewhere else. The only one we know who can split his essence many times and not be diminished is Jesus. Some entities who are higher up can trilocate, which means they can be three places at once. Jesus can split his essence and be many places at once. I myself can only bilocate. I can be attending a lecture and still be with Sylvia. Most everybody in spirit form can bilocate, so they can be doing something and still attend to their loved one. Are we omnipresent with you? Yes! We never leave you.

Many times, an entity will petition for you, but you meet the person and do not find them to be compatible with your chart. You have a right, then, to choose another guide. Sylvia and I did not know each other in any life. We had never really met each other.

I can tell you honestly when Sylvia first met me, she really did not, what you call, love me from the bottom of her heart. She thought I was very stiff and too formal. We did not hit it off at first. But I practiced so long to be a communicating guide, and I have been with her for so long that we have bonded with each other. I have been with her since the time of her birth. In that time, you become so very close through shared adversity, pain, sadness, joy, and love; such a friendship develops over time, and once that bond is made, we become like kindred souls and are never again split apart.

Do you know that each one of you have a special name on the Other Side? It is the name that we go by. Let me give you an example of this. Sylvia's name on the Other Side is Elizabeth, but she is well known throughout all the quadrants as "Bun." It is a nickname referring to a life of hers in England when she loved hot cross buns. These little idiosyncrasies come over with us, and people are known by their nicknames. This familiarity is a sign of love.

How do we get our name on the Other Side?

We actually choose it, or a lot of times it just comes about because of something the entity fancies. As far back as I can remember, I have always kept the same name, which is actually Iena, where Francine was Sylvia's interpretation. It seems to have always been with me; there was no gigantic billboard displaying it. I seem to have always known my name.

I never want to give you the idea that the Other Side stands on formality. We are very loving, congenial, and respectful of each other, but we do not stand on any of the formalities that even you do in your world. Our manners are impeccable. We do not intrude on each other, but there is a loving camaraderie that pervades our daily life.

Do guides share knowledge?

Oh, yes! That is why, so many times, when you are watching someone that is sick, even though you have never felt that way, you can almost assimilate that pain with certain people.

We can permit our guide to read our minds. How long does that last?

You should give them sanction for your entire incarnate lifetime; otherwise, you have to do it every time. The privacy between God and you is inviolate; we cannot butt into that. When God is speaking to you, and God does, a veil falls that we cannot intercept. You would be surprised how many times in a day God speaks to you. We will see this golden cloud mass descend over you, which means—and this is the most beautiful part of it—that God's ear has now come down. It envelops you. We stand back with our head bowed while you communicate with your Creator. When you do pray—every time—this beautiful, shiny rainbow cloud comes down.

There is nothing worse than a person giving sanction for one day. Then the guide must try to figure out what is going on with the person. I have had that terrible situation with Sylvia yelling at me, "Why didn't you know I was worried about such and such?" I said, "I cannot read your mind." She thought she had given me sanction for a whole lifetime when she had not.

You must say to us that we are allowed to have unconditional access to your mind at all times. This does not mean that we are invading it, but that we are able to read it. However, anytime you are talking to your Creator, your guide cannot hear it.

Is it difficult for you to enter our world?

Yes. Your atmosphere is so dense. It is so thick, very much like going into a swamp. I am probably more fortunate because I can come into a body to communicate. But if I were not in a body, it would be 50 times harder to make contact. Also, your gravitational pull is harder. There is no other planet in which aging occurs like it does here.

How do you perceive time on the Other Side?

I do not know time, and I do not know how to explain to you that I only see time when I am communicating via Sylvia. The reason why you know time is because you have the sunrise, sunset, seasons, and so on. Anybody who has experienced solitary confinement can begin to understand the feeling of timelessness—but I do not want to give you the idea that the Other Side is like solitary confinement! When there is no time, the marvelous thing is there is *no rush.* You do not realize what an enemy time is. It causes the frustrating feeling of not having accomplished what you had wished to—of missing the boat, the party, the wedding, or the right person. Everything for you hinges on this miserable pendulum swinging.

Is it better to make an appointment with our guides?

Yes, because then we know and are ready to go to work. It is so hard for us to understand what your time concept is, so when you say to meet you at a certain time, it is much easier for us. The other night Sylvia was trying to go to sleep, and I was talking to her. Her time did not mean anything to me, except I realized that she wanted to go to sleep. I have a problem with that because we do not have to sleep.

Are there stars on the Other Side?

Oh, yes. Absolutely. We can go beyond that atmosphere up to what is called the Rocky Mountains on your side. We pierce above the veil then, and look out into the whole universe. We love to go to the mountains. We do not walk. We "think" ourselves there. We can go anywhere and look above this atmosphere, which hangs a little lower than yours does.

Can you go anywhere in the universe?

Yes, anyplace you want, including the Akashic Records. If you are very interested in studying historical events, you can go back and experience right there at that time in the living state. You would appear as a person of that day. You do not know how many people you have met who are really ghosts in your world; they are Akashic Record experiencers. You know how people will walk around saying, "Whatever happened to so-and-so?" No one knows, because that entity was here from another place.

Can we access the future in the Akashic Records?

Yes, and God, by knowing it, puts it in His "now." It is accessible until you pull down your own chart. Now there are modifications to this, but the overall concept will stay the same. Everything is happening in God's now.

Can guides administer to us physically?

We are able to "knock you out." A small pinch on the bottom of your foot usually signals that you have been given "a shot" by your guide. We can give shots of energy or healing boosts. We can do it through a shot, or if you have been under severe stress or have lost energy and need rejuvenation, a beam of light.

How do our guides communicate with us?

They will tap and pop, whistle, call your name, wiggle the bed, and do anything they can to get your attention. They will even pop radio waves. If you tune your radio to a dead space, they can make almost a stiletto sound. Believe me, they would never do anything to scare you. If they do, just say, "Cut it out. You can do it another way. I hear you, but you don't have to wiggle the bed."

I will tell you how far we can go. You can literally ask—now this is really going to put me up for suspicion, but I will say it anyway— you can even ask for a message to be given to you through lights. While driving home, you can say to Father or Mother God or the Archetypes, "If the answer to my question is yes, let me see a car with one light. If it is no, let me see high beams." We can actually manipulate light. We can do it in your house, even with the faucet—two drips mean no, one drip means yes. We can flick lights because we are electrical beings. The purpose is to let you know that we are still around. We are saying, "Hi, we are here."

Can we communicate with our guides through handwriting?

Oh, yes. I am much more supportive of automatic writing than of Ouija boards, which are surrounded by negative energy—please do not touch them. The dark entities just manipulate those. Your hands are pure, but Ouija boards have been used for so many nasty, bad things that they are telephones that should never be used.

Is it okay to use tarot cards?

You can, as long as you keep blessing them. You always think only priests can bless. How ridiculous! Anybody can bless. Say, "Go with my blessing." Bless your children. You have the power from God to bless everyone.

❦ ❦ ❦

"Everyone who is really a seeker after their own truth is a Gnostic."
— Francine

"Disbelief and skepticism are all right.
Stupid *is not all right!"*
— Sylvia

❦ ❦ ❦ ❦ ❦ ❦

Metaphysical Universe

Francine: In addition to the physical, I want to address the metaphysical universe. The physical universe is made up of the molecular structure that is held by the hand of God. It is nothing more than a schoolyard in which everybody comes into these vehicles called bodies that have brain-pods ready to be manipulated by the spirit. The extraterrestrials are part of the physical universe.

The metaphysical universe includes all the mansions of God, all the levels, schematics, Other Sides, Archetypes, Councils, and even the hierarchy of the Nuvoites. There must be another name by which we could refer to this, except for the fact that if you used the word *mystical,* everyone takes it as something that is beyond grasping. So for want of a better word, we will stay with *metaphysical,* referring to the spiritual world, which is the true, eternal world.

Nuvo

Nuvo is the giant, conglomerate Other Side. It is at the center—right at the heart or the chest of what we call the Great Man (see Chapter 1). There are seven quite beautiful, fascinating, and wondrous rings around it. There are four levels to each ring.

Nuvo is beyond this planet's Other Side and does not have a physical, living side. People do not go to the planet of Nuvo and live a life and die—no. People just go directly to Nuvo. It is exactly in the center of the universe—an actual place, not a mystical one.

Nuvoites, by their very nature, are messenger entities. It sometimes takes them many lifetimes to converge, because they are the truest Gnostics in the world. Jesus was a Nuvoite. Nuvoites are sent out on a mission of knowledge.

Everything advances from Nuvo all the way down through the different galactic orders, down to the very tail end that we call "the rim of horror." Then it ascends backward toward its home, which is that pinpoint of light, way far away, at the very center. When you die, your tunnel does not go straight through to Nuvo; instead, it goes straight to this planet's Other Side. You stay there for a while to reorient yourself. Then you might want to go back to the Pleiades, Andromeda, or any other planet's Other Side to which you have been, lived and died on, and want to visit. This might become your ultimate home, where all your loved ones may follow you as you wish. If they are not Nuvoites, they must stay on their own Other Side. You may visit them, come down to them, stay close to them, but here is the rub—they cannot follow you. Now, do not be distressed by that because time is a twinkling. The reason they cannot follow you is that their course of advancement is different.

Nuvoites are special, inner-circle people who were chosen from the very beginning of time to come together, to congregate and be blessed as messengers from God, white knights, warriors, holy soldiers truly searching for the Grail.

By the way, the Grail is nothing more than the cup of knowledge. That is all it was. It was not the cup that Jesus drank from. He said, "Seek and ye shall find. Knock and it shall be opened unto you." Do not just sit there like dummies, is what he said to his apostles. Do not just sit there and expect it to be fed to you. Almost all of his messages were either metaphysical or practical, but the metaphysical words were ruled out. Some of his parables were absolutely the most ethereal, metaphysical words ever spoken.

Most of his message was, "Enter into your own heart, and you will find eternal salvation and happiness." This wondrous word *save* that goes around has become such an off-word. There is no soul that is not "saved"; it sounds like something else is thrown away. There is no one who is lost. How much "saving" do you want? You are the one who saves and savors the knowledge, the insightfulness, and the lifting of your soul. You can only do that through knowledge and experience.

With knowledge, people are brought to their own level of salvation. That is what true salvation means. The Nuvoites will start rising up and migrating toward you. Nuvoites make a strong warrior band. They are not so interested, trust me, in saving the world—although that is part of it; it is more important to harvest souls.

The Pleiades are almost like a way-station, because people are constantly going in and out as rescuers to other planetary systems. From Earth, most of you will go to the Pleiades on a rescue mission, which is in itself a learning process. Then you go out to other places and pick up souls that need to be brought to the light. From the Pleiades, people go out to other areas such as Crab Nebula and Andromeda, which may be dark little planets, and save the people incarnated there. There is one area in Andromeda that is totally desolate. You can think of it as a place where the prisoners of other places have been sent, much like how Australia used to be. A lot of these souls are lost, until they are rescued by those from the Pleiades. So there is much work to be done.

Archetypes

The metaphysical universe contains all things unseen. This encompasses the whole hierarchy of the Archetypes, who are pure energy forces that come directly from God; they never incarnate. The Bible spoke about them as Archangels, but that is not totally correct. They are all golden and blonde in color, and they seem androgynous, but they take on very much of the male figure, the eunuch in sexuality. They are pure love and pure protection. I can give you many names of Archetypes, and not just the Archangels' names that are mentioned in the Bible—such as Michael, Orion, Ariel, Raphael, and Gabriel—but thousands of other names if we had enough time to sit and go through them. Those are the primary Archangels who were delegated to healing or protection.

Whenever you get into a mental, physical, or spiritual bind, it would behoove you to call on the Archetypes. They have been known—by the power of their energy alone—to literally keep cars from hitting you if you are driving, or dislodge or misdirect a knife that would be hurled at you. I am sure that when you've been driving and have been convinced that a car would hit you, or one had come so close that, as the slang goes, "another coat of paint" and it would have had you, that this is when the Archetypes have literally dimensionalized the whole polarity of space and removed the object.

Archetypes are always for protection. Every day you should ask your Archetypes to surround you. They love it and are very unobtrusive guides. They are probably the only guides that must be asked to be around—unless there is real danger; then they come immediately, almost like, what you call in your world, a paramedic.

Do they alter time or space?

Sylvia was saved from a car wreck by Archetypes; they put her in a different position. You know that everything in your molecular, physical world is moving. You know that the chair you are seated on, the floor beneath your feet, and the ceiling above you are all moving. Even though it seems to be stable, the molecules in everything move. Now what makes it so remarkable is that each pipe has its "pipeness"—in other words, the molecules of the pipe do not become the wood of the speakers. For that reason alone, it seems to be stationary. It maintains its identity. Aristotle defined *essence* as that without which a thing cannot exist.

Now you say, "If two wood things were together, why do they not leak over and meld?" They do not. Each keeps its stationary, molecular form. That, my dear friends, is probably one of the greatest miracles wrought by God! You can see how specifically perfect God's mind is. If something is supposed to be a picture frame, it remains a picture frame. It is held there by the thought of God. Now that in itself is a total miracle!

You have wonderful molecular *devas*. The ancient sages of India used this term to refer to demigods, but everything in nature, animate or inanimate, contains in it a spirit or spirits called devas. This chair, your car, any vehicle contains the molecular structure of a deva. It is hard to believe that in their own realm or dominion, they are like mini, breathing gods. In this universe, there is a stacked elevation of beings. So all animate and inanimate objects are in their own phylum. Nothing is ever lost.

In this world everything is held; the Archetypes are able to decompress the molecular structure of something, shrinking or expanding it. After all, they are from the metaphysical world, in which such things are possible. So people will say to you, "How did I fall eight stories and live? I was in a crash—how did I live?" On and on it goes. It is because it was not their time. They still had to learn something, so the Archetypes altered the molecular structure.

Archetypes work outside our time frame?

They can even transmute energy to the point that they can defray bad people or any evil coming toward you. The whole crux lies in the fact that you must call on them! The amazing thing about spirituality is that it will never invade you. You must ask for it! No one has ever had spirituality rise up unless something in the mind rose up to meet it.

I think that is where so many churches got the idea that you must *ask* to be "saved." There is no such thing as being "saved." But you must *ask* for the Archetypes to help you, the God-Centeredness to come, your guides to be around you, and your God-centeredness to be intact. For all this you must ask! If you do not, it does not come. But on the other hand, darkness can invade anywhere. The treachery of this world is that there are no rules to darkness. Dark entities or energy can creep in under floors, under doors. This is their toy box—their world of prejudice, ignorance, and greed.

Sylvia has always asked for the Archetypes. You have to realize that she had the knowledge years ago. You don't have to ask for them every time—just say, "For the rest of my life, I want a band of Archetypes to be around me." They do not forget. Whatever you speak out now or ask for, is for eternity.

Who directs the Archetypes?

Mother God. They are Her direct army. We have talked about the fact that everything, ultimately, was made by Her. But there are certain parts of the universe that are more relegated to Him, such as the static holding of everything physical. She is action, movement, dynamics, love. So the Archetypes are much more, I guess you might say for want of a better term, Her army, Her cohorts, Her servants, as it were. Even when the world did not accept Her, and believed in Archangels, they still were directly addressing Her.

Way back when I was a girl in life, my Aztec-Incan community had total belief in and reciprocation with the Mother Goddess. But guess what? One of the reasons why the conquistadores wanted to annihilate us was because they thought we were pagan. It has been that way from the very beginning. All the ancient religions paid total homage to Her.

How many times, here in life, have we taken an emotion to unnecessary extremes? I did in my short lifetime. I created more fear for myself than I needed because the conquistadores were coming. For two years, I could have been enjoying my life, but instead I was consumed by fear that they would come, which they finally did. Of course, I was killed by a spear, but I often think of the two years I could have enjoyed myself before that. When the spear finally struck, I did not feel anything. I left my body immediately.

Did Satan tempt Jesus?

No. That was an allegory showing that anyone who is a messenger, and had the following that Jesus had, could be tempted by greed at some point. Look at some of the televangelists—their greed! So that was a metaphor or allegory, saying, "Look at what you could have if you turn from God." Of course, Jesus was tempted, but not by Satan. When anyone was tempted, they always thought it was Satan. It was not Satan. In the first place, a dark entity does not go around anybody who is truly for people anyway. But you must realize that 40 days and nights in the desert can be very hallucinatory—you are dehydrated and delusional. Jesus never once lied about anything. It is those who wrote about him who lied! He was very much into truth, consciousness, and goodness. The tragedy is that people later lost the truth about him.

Satan is a misunderstood concept because it really refers to a *state* of being rather than an *actual* being. Anyone can easily attain the level of Satan, not only by being a dark entity from the "start," but by being gray. The dark and the white were created; the grayness is in evolvement. You will know the gray entities immediately because you will never know how to read them or how to figure them out, and with the least provocation, they turn dark.

Why does the Bible say to fear God?

That is the greatest tragedy and such a terrible darkness. The concept of a vengeful god is a complete falsehood; it separates people from God. The one true "sin," if you want to call it that, is despair. That is what darkness lives off of.

The Council and Your Chart

The Council members are also called the master teachers. This is a fancy way to say the same thing. I don't know why everybody has to have fancy words for everything, such as the Ascended Masters or the White Brotherhood. Really, what the White Brotherhood referred to were the Gnostics. Either one was synonymous. The elders, the master teachers, are the Council.

The Council have always been a group of people that help you on your chart. When you decide what life you want to come into, the

Council helps pick the geographical location, what you need to do, what theme you have to perfect, what you would want to retract if you got in a bind, and what would be the consequences of that karma. All this is delineated before you come in.

How long does planning a life take?

Probably in your time, as close as I can get with the mathematicians helping me, is 80 years for one life interconnecting. But it goes so fast in our time.

Now before you come in, there is a very wide network of Council and spirit guides. And many times, Mother God has intercepted and said, "You don't want to go there. You might prefer to do this." So you were counseled extensively. All of you went through tremendous counseling, not only in a lot of lifetimes, but especially this one! Especially coming into a Gnostic situation—that took a lot of counseling, the whole aspect of every single life. That is why a lot of times we see miscarriages. The soul has decided that the parent has taken, maybe, a wrong turn or it is not going to fulfill the theme properly, so the entity retracts. Same thing with abortion.

Is abortion okay?

What I want to say is only logical, and has nothing to do with murder or harming a child or a life. What no one on your planet understands is that no one on my Side is stupid. No entity will enter a fetus that is going to get emptied out. We just do not do that. There is nothing to learn from that.

Why do children die?

To incur perfection for the people left. God is in service to us, we are in service to God, and each of us is in service to each other.

With a miscarriage, will the same soul reenter later?

It can, absolutely. We have seen this a lot. A mother will mis-carry and then that same entity will come in when the fetus is healthy or ready enough to. We have even seen small babies (what you call babies are really full-grown entities in a baby body) die from Sudden Infant Death Syndrome (SIDS), then come right back in as the next baby. SIDS is often due to unexpected changes in the circumstances of birth or family, to a degree that the entity cannot properly fulfill their chart, so they simply leave the body and wait for more favorable con-ditions.

What about those having trouble conceiving?

Your culture has made people think they *must* have children. The problem is when the chart is written, everything is fine, everything is wondrous. On the Other Side, you made your chart, but in life you modify, excuse, lather over, sneak under, and go above; that does not mean you are going off-chart. You still always manage to get there. On the Other Side, it's easy to say what you will not do. Then you get down here, and unfortunately you get religiously, culturally, and socially brainwashed.

Does a mother know when a soul enters her baby?

Yes, a mother knows when the "quickening" happens. I will bet that every mother knew almost the exact point in time that she con-ceived, and was also pretty sure of exactly when the quickening happened.

Immediately, when the soul drops in, a silver cord that we call the "parachute cord" is attached. At the same time, little electrical fire-works go off in the brain of the baby. Pregnant mothers have got to be the happiest people in the world—in spite of morning sickness— because they are carrying such divinity inside. It is a shame that so many of you carried your children and did not know any of this. You knew it was a blessing to have your baby and you carried it inside you and all those wondrous things, but following the process of how this divine intervention comes about is truly such a blessed event. We never get tired of watching it.

Does the soul have a brain?

That is a very interesting question. You have a mind-soul that resides in the physiological makeup of the gray matter. The physiological gray matter is only a host. It is beautiful to watch the soul enter the tiny vehicle; immediately there is a spark inside the gray matter. All of a sudden, the brain becomes alive. We constantly stand and watch this. Sparklers go off in the brain; it is truly amazing.

Can we go against the Council?

Many do, and do you know how that usually ends up? Suicide. You must take into consideration the individual stubbornness of every being. We have seen it time and time again—someone will say, "I know better," and the Council will say, "No, you don't." They get in way over their heads in life and just cannot take it. It's an escape route that backfires, but they should not be judged either. No one should be judged.

A suicide comes back instantly?

Yes, and then they have to complete another, almost identical situation. Once you have bitten it off, you have to chew it. Very much like you have to take English to graduate. You are going to have to take it again and again until you pass it.

Suicide is the most selfish act possible. It is the only warp that appears anywhere. A person who is susceptible to suicide has usually committed suicide in past lives, is ready to do it again, has been counseled not to come down, but does it anyway. It is the ultimate, "It's on your shoulders, not mine. I leave it with you out of anger and heartache."

However, when you get ready to die, you have every right to say,

"I do not want artificial means to keep me alive." That is one of the tenets of our religion. We are absolutely within our rights to say, "Let God's will be done." Too many times, I think, we have a hard time saying good-bye to people. Say to them, "You can go!"

Does one suicide mandate multiple reincarnations?

We have heard of that; it has happened, but not that often. It depends on what the karmic retribution was—on how many souls they left hysterically wondering, "What did I do?" You see, suicide really is the ultimate slap in the face to those left behind.

In some cases, I have seen as many as 20 extra lives get tacked on to a person who has committed suicide. They have to experience almost the same basic trials and tribulations, such as an alcoholic father, and so on. They have got to go through the same thing again. There is no free pass.

Now let us address one exception to the rule of retributive karma for suicide. Let us say someone has a serious and terminal condition, such as a brain tumor, and the whole pituitary gland or synaptic impulses have gone haywire. The person's mind is just being flooded by what we see as an alien fluid, so to speak, or let us say a chemical. Then we are talking about a biochemical infringement—a fluke. Amazingly enough, the person has also picked that. But that is still hard, because all the person's loved ones are still left.

Is an accidental drug overdose a suicide?

Yes, absolutely. They have created their own fake chemical imbalance. That is entirely different from a genetic imbalance that might have come from a psychotic parent.

How quickly is a suicide sent back?

We catch them at the tunnel and send them right back down. They do not even get to reach the Other Side.

How can another, similar life be planned so quickly?

Are you kidding? Within the universe, there are a myriad of identical or closely identical lives. It does not have to be on the same continent. It can be on another one. You know yourself that when you meet and talk to people even in your own sphere, you say, "This person had the exact same family situation as I did." There are a million such identifications.

How can we help someone die?

Counsel them; tell them to let go. It is very effective to tell them to "let go of the cord." We have found them dangling there and holding on to that cord. It is amazing, too, as the soul drops in, that there is a silver cord. As they go out, the cord becomes gold. We have a lot of ways to tell when a soul is coming over. A blue light begins to flash, almost like a train coming in. We have a giant board that also shows the approach of an incoming soul.

What is amazing is that we have seen blue lights flashing for two years or more. They are stubbornly refusing to come over, just hanging on. They just will not let go of the cord. They just keep suffering and suffering. They will not go. You do not have to be a doctor to realize that there is nothing left anymore to keep hanging on to. Everybody knows somebody like that. It becomes that simple. They do not want to go—despite all the pain, chemotherapy, radiation, etc.

What about euthanasia?

No, we are not for that at all, although we do not judge. Now if you are going to talk somebody over, that is a different thing—that is wonderful! We are pulling one way and you are pushing the other. Sometimes that is the only way to get them to go, but do not use any external means. Then you get into a very strange moral paradox, because now you are going to be responsible for taking a life—you are deciding who should go.

Consequently, those who do this are going to have to come back and go through the same type of thing. It absolutely is a suicide. However, it is perfectly acceptable to say, "I do not want any life-preserving measures." That is fine. You have every right to say that. What you are doing is removing any artificial means, but you are not injecting anything. The minute you start an invasive technique in the body, then you are in spiritual trouble. The only thing we do not like about the whole abortion issue is that there is an invasive technique. Now certainly the entity is not going to enter in, but we do not like the invasive technique in the body.

Do we plan our own death?

We all do conglomerately for perfection. Now those are very definitive things. Let us say the mother decided that she will linger for ten years. The daughter is going to make sure she learns from her or whomever it might be. It is a conglomerate decision to learn. "You run the race, and I'll stand by and cheer," or whatever it might be. You get to be the victim, and I will be the persecutor. It's a tradeoff. Usually, the person who takes a long, lingering death is not the one who is learning. The ones left standing around are learning.

Can our deceased loved ones come around us?

In the whole metaphysical universe, all the loved ones who have passed come around as helpers—now that is a crowd! Not only people you have known from this life, but from all your lives. So you can imagine what kind of a crowd you walk around with. You are the warriors. You are the ones who are off to battle! All of us over here are living this really luxurious, wonderful life. The least we can do is to give you help. We know what a battlefield you are on. Any bullet-proof jacket you can wear, any kind of camouflage you can put on, anything you can do to protect yourself from this battlefield until you get to safety, is fine with us.

Does a dark entity have any good aspects?

Please be aware that a truly dark entity is highly defined. It is not a person who is simply in a bad mood, or even someone who goes insane and has a psychotic episode. Even that does not necessarily indicate a dark entity. A dark entity is truly the highest form of sociopathic personality. There is no guilt or remorse, no depth of love or any feeling. They are almost like cyborgs; they have hard, dead eyes and a rigid demeanor. They can be charming, but everything is metallic about them. They are uncaring and greedy, and they step on everyone.

All they have is their incarnations—generation after generation, they never make it to the Other Side. They learn all manner of wily ways. You have heard people say, "No matter how far and how deep I looked, I could not find a good thing about this person." That is a dark entity! Do they have abusive childhoods? Sometimes. But sometimes they have perfect childhoods.

Do we chart dark entities as our children?

Oh, certainly. Many times dark entities will come through white ones, or white will come through dark. I cannot think of a better or more horrific test than for a white entity to be born of a dark one, or vice versa. Here in your midst you have this "bad seed" running around.

They take their toll on you. White entities will be accosted by these dark entities. They will come as a group, or even come in as a child or parent to a white entity. A white entity will always have some dark entity in their midst with whom they must do battle. There are groups of dark entities who will face you in your life. It does not take very long for them to show their hand. You do not have to wait for years and years.

When you are writing your chart, you will deliberately pick a dark entity to be in your midst for you to learn from. A dark entity is pretty much a shallow drum. They are guarded and driven by a dark force and seem to be almost totally sociopathic, borderline people. They do not seem to have any consciousness within themselves. They are totally bent toward destruction. Drugs are the dark force's friend, or anything that puts the soul out of control. This makes it possible for you to be attacked. Unhealthy amounts of alcohol or illicit drugs leave you exposed. I do not mean you cannot have a social drink. Do you know that on our side we have actual parties in which we do have a clicking of wine glasses and a drinking of wine?

As you advance spiritually, you will be tested on every ground you can. When we talk about a battlefield, there are many parts of the strategic battle that you have to go into—not only the bomb squad, but the infantry and air force. Otherwise, how can you know, to your highest form of perfection, what the length and breadth of your soul can be? Many entities do not take on the dark until they have become seasoned. But you see, zealousness takes over.

We see many entities petitioning, "I can handle that. Yes, and I will take that on, too!" Then they get down here and realize they were unrealistically brave. But it is very understandable, because they were in a perfect, euphoric, beautiful environment. Of course they thought they could handle anything—but that is where the danger lies. We counsel people, "Yes, you feel so great today, but when you go in, it is not going to be that way." They think they could never forget what they know on my side, but they do.

Do Gnostics take on more than usual?

Always, always, always! But I will tell you one thing about Gnostics: They have the backbone to withstand it. No matter how much they are battered around, they do not usually succumb. We usually—and this is not to make you feel special—but we do not argue with Gnostics as much as with other people, because Gnostics are very well trained. They have been through many battles. So we are talking about the elite forces. If you saw some of the battles you have been through—the Crusades and being thrown to the lions—you would know you could handle a lot.

Are there different levels of white entities?

There are. There are the mystical traveler entities, and just plain white entities. There are less evolved ones, but they are all good. They are just babyfied. The only ones you can judge are the dark entities. Believe me, you will not have to sit here and write out a list of what they are. If you ever get entangled by one of those, you know it! You are going to know it real fast.

How do dark entities affect us?

They know every single emotional trigger point you have. You see the best weapon they have is to play on your emotions. The biggest one they can use, and their favorite, is despair. They are more apt to be there at a time when you are the most down. Strangely enough, when there is a big upsurge of joy or a big movement in Gnosticism, the dark will rise up to meet it. You can certainly block it. Jesus said time and time again, "Be alert. Be aware. Be watchful." Every morning, say, "I want the Archetypes to surround me." Even though you have said it as a blanket command, say, "I do not want to be besieged by dark entities!"

Do the Archetypes come quickly?

Immediately! For as long as the darkness stays. They can stay around you all the time, but then they will ask for other troops. Many times when you get depressed or down, or you get a feeling of futility, ask first, "If this is my own thought, my own mind working, then let that be rinsed clean. If it is coming from outside myself, let the Archetypes come." Ask for a rinsing, a cleansing of your mind. It might be something biochemical going on with you that you can ask to be corrected. Most people are not biochemically predisposed to this; rather, they are susceptible to being badgered by dark entities until a chemical imbalance is created.

Are children more open to dark entities?

No. Because they are so fresh from the Other Side, they almost carry a heavenly glow with them. By the time a child reaches about ten, though, it really begins to wear thin, unless the child is a dark entity, and then they start out right away.

Children are usually aware of all manner of extra- and ultraterrestrials and also dark entities. That is why when a child says to you, "Mommy, I do not like him or her," you ought to listen. Even if it is Aunt Bertha whom everybody loved. If they say, "Mommy, that is a mean man or lady," then take notice!

Who controls the dark entities?

No one—they are out of control. If they were in control, we would not have any problems. We do not have any problems with dark entities on my side, because Earth is their habitat. We know we are sending you down here into nothing but darkness!

How do some abused children stay healthy?

Because they are white entities, so they cannot turn dark. Whether you can forgive, or give it to God to forgive, it does not matter. Sylvia said at one point, "Why was I supposed to go through so many things? Couldn't I have just read about it?" I said to her, "If you had not experienced it, you would not have had the same empathy." She was mad at me for a week! Yet I would say the same to you. You were meant to become sweeter, more magnanimous and loving, more feminine and emotional because of it.

You are talking about an entity's relative strength or weakness. White entities do not turn; however, they can go through the throes of problems or even addictions. Sometimes we have seen white entities go through addiction, but they come out of it. But it is the continued use that is a form of suicide. Drink yourself to death; take drugs until you are half-crazy. It is a way to cop out of life; that is why we are so against it. When you take too much alcohol or too many drugs into your system, you lower your resistance—and guess who comes around in full force? Dark entities.

Now I do not mean that you cannot go out and have a few glasses of wine or do a few things for fun. But when you are half-stupid and crazed, then you are opening the door to all dark influences, almost like turning on a light and having them all rush at you. That is why people say, "I drank, and I cannot believe I was capable of doing such and such." Of course you were not. Dark entities were manipulating your mind as if you were a mannequin. Even certain medical treatments cause this.

Is a long-term alcoholic a suicide?

Yes, absolutely. They have deadened their life; they haven't even lived it. They just put themselves under anesthesia. Notice how many young people you have on drugs. That is because you have a mass rush to get in here. They are not taking as much counseling and therapy as they should before they get in. They all want to perfect so they are coming in, biting off more than they can chew.

Is a functional alcoholic committing suicide?

It does not make any difference. They are not really functioning. I don't care what you see—they are still not fully in there. They are not really at work. Think of what they could do if they were sober. They are what we call the "maintenance drinker."

Can we "hide out" for a while?

That is rest. There is nothing against curling up, crawling in, and covering over—that is fine. I am talking about the morbidity of constantly focusing on, "I am sick, I am tired, I have a headache, my neck hurts, I have a legal battle, I am upset," and on and on. Morbid, miserable whining is a fruitful field for the dark.

Can we let the Archetypes battle the dark?

Absolutely. Here is what you do: Mentally step out of their path and say to the Archetypes, "You get them." It is very much like watching a big brother come in and bash somebody to pieces, while you go off and relax. You just do not get into it. In spirit, you are strong. If you were in spirit form, you could do this without help, but you are playing on their dirty turf. When you take yourself away in this manner, a dark entity can actually almost implode on itself. Instead of empowering them, you take away their power. You empower yourself. When you do this, you ask for feminine energy, whether you are male or female. Literally, you ask for feminine power because it is the militant power on this planet.

When you empower yourself with feminine energy, you can call on the male attribute to hold steady, but it will anyway. Call on the feminine principle to get in and fight. Do not be afraid to say at any given point, "Now Azna, you come in!" People say, "She cannot." No. If you do not ask, you are not going to get it. Dark entities are like a virus!

These entities, as bad as they are, are still experiencing darkness. As such, God is experiencing through them. At the very end of things, though—and this just shows you how loving and just God is, and that there is no hell—God will absorb these entities back into the Uncreated Mass and purify them. When you are going to the Other Side, dark entities go to the left, as it were; they are recycled and go right back into life again.

The golden and white tunnel goes straight off, and that door is sealed to them. So the tunnel that shoots from you to the Other Side is protected. I do not care how many people say that as you are going through this, demons are clawing at you and trying to pull you. That is a most ridiculous thing!

Feminine energy can be frightening, too.

When I talk about the feminine principle, please do not misinterpret this information. I am not talking about women. That is entirely different. Strangely enough, what has always been a fear is that when the feminine principle rises up, it could be just as vicious as patriarchy ever was unless we keep both sides balanced. That is why Gnostics have, with their whole lives, been so absolutely strong about supporting both the Father and the Mother.

It is true that when the feminine principle goes awry, even in the animal kingdom, it is far more vicious. But do not use that to interpret what you are seeing. The feminist movement has nothing to do with the feminine principle, although it might have been a bit like John the Baptist heralding that something was coming. Anything pushed to its extreme becomes almost a caricature of itself. Patriarchy, when pushed to its extreme, becomes dominating, macho, and egotistical. Femininity, when pushed too far, becomes petty, conniving, and insidious. Anything pushed to its ultimate becomes, many times, the opposite of what it should be, without balance. That is in the physical realm rather than the metaphysical.

Now, here is one thing you must guard against: Women, you are not being kind or giving enough to your male counterparts. Please, you must have sympathy, understanding, caring, and love. Even a morose man does not come close to the moroseness of a woman. Do not get too carried away with that. We are seeing it more with relationships. Women are really becoming very venomous with their counterparts.

This also occurs in business and work relationships. The strange thing about women is that they want so much, yet they really go after men's egos. In case no one ever explained this to you, men's egos are far more fragile than women's will ever be! They cannot ever take the hurt and the humanistic abuse that a woman can take. A man criticizes a woman, but if she criticizes him back, she will destroy him. Is that fair? Of course not. But it is the way the sexes were made on this planet. On the Other Side, there is no such thing as pettiness or morbidity. We have seen more and more of that here, and it is not right for a man to be cruel, vindictive, and critical of a woman. I do not mean to take sides. I am just saying that, with the mass amount of feminine energy that is coming up, you must be on guard against going too far.

How can we balance our relationships?

Women's spirituality is rising, and the poor men are like dunder-heads walking behind them saying, "What is going on?" Ask the Archetypes to infuse them; sometimes you have to say to a man, as you have done in many lifetimes, "If you do not follow me, I will have to leave you." I am not for anybody breaking up, but sometimes you just have to. As you get brighter and lighter, many times the person who is with you gets frightened. It's like when one person gets thin-ner or fatter, and others think, *Oh my goodness, they are growing away from me.* Yes, it is true, they are!

I think that rather than being vengeful and hateful, it is so much better if you just leave. When the time comes and you know that something has ended, why keep see-sawing back and forth? That is karmic torture for both people. If you have found that the person you are with is really beyond any point that you can deal with them, why not let them go so they can find their own perfection?

The more a person advances spiritually, the more they realize that this life is only a passing shadow. That does not mean I don't want you to concentrate on your love life, business, and health problems, but it is all so transient. It is only a short stay at school. You may not like the dormitory, you may not like the meals, but you will gradu-ate—I guarantee it. No one has ever regressed. Do not stay in situa-tions that you cannot tolerate. It hinders your spiritual growth. You may fear that you will hurt someone by leaving them—but are you hurting them more by staying on? I am not advocating a mass split-ting of marriages and partnerships, but too many people on your plane stay on endlessly with a person or situation because they are misguided. "If I leave, what will they do without me?" Well, they may actually start to live their own life.

Can we teach children Gnostic philosophy?

Even though it is a little bit advanced, it is not over their heads. Children understand more, because they are so fresh. Look at that mother's child who said, "I have my spirit guides and my masters inside me." This is a small child.

Years ago, when Sylvia had time to teach the little children about their spirit guides and the White Light, every child said, "Yes, I know." Not one challenged her. They instantly know because you are speaking truth from the Other Side. If you start telling them about hellfire, damnation, and Adam and Eve, then what does that do? What do children care about Adam and Eve? What is that going to help them with?

If you have not felt a certain stirring in your soul, you will. I am told by the Council that each soul is now beginning to be called. What we call "the voice in the soul" wants to come forward and enter the circle of light. I am told that each soul will respond to this in their own way, out of the terrible darkness in which some of you have walked. But the stirrings of the soul are now going to be stronger than they have ever been and call you against all odds to come into the circle of light. I can see it all around me. It becomes a small seed, and all of a sudden it bursts open as a flower. Once it becomes a flower, you will never, ever go back to anything else.

Are there any conditions put on you? Do you have to "buy" your way into the inner circle? Of course not! Do you have to buy your way into each level? No. It is something that happens individually within your soul. You give your heart and soul—as Sylvia has done—to this belief and to the growth of this movement, against all odds, asking nothing from anyone except coming together in a power circle. That is all. In the power circle, the soul elevates, depression leaves, you are not going to need drugs or drink, and you will lose a lot of your infirmities. This must get started so each person will lend their power to the concentration of light. Then convalescent hospitals will spring up, and children and the homeless will be fed and cared for. In the inner circle of light, the petals of the flower spring out powerfully. That is enough to live your life for. If nothing else, make your mark by building this. Then, forever after, people will come without fear and not have to give away all their worldly possessions. That is ridiculous. People should live, eat, breathe, and take care of their children. No one has to live in a cubicle and eat brown rice. That is an atrocity before God!

Feel and listen, and see if your soul is not stirring. See if the dedication of your heart grows. Because what happens is, God's finger does move. When God's finger touches you, that is the salve, the balm. All the pain goes away.

Seven Levels of the Other Side

Sylvia: Earlier, we discussed the seven schematics of creation. As Francine likes to say, there are levels within levels. Following are the seven levels of the Other Side incurred by life knowledge.

1. The first level is a way-station for inbound and outbound souls.
2. The second level holds orientation and the Hall of Wisdom.
3. The third level is for animal husbandry and taking care of plants and flowers.
4. The fourth level is for artistic pursuits.
5. The fifth level holds the mission life entities.
6. The sixth level are the teachers and researchers.
7. The seventh level is returning to the Uncreated Mass.

The Seventh Level on the Other Side

Francine: Now, let us talk about the seventh level on my side—returning to the Uncreated Mass. It is quite an amazing phenomenon, probably the most beautiful thing that any of us ever gets to experience. In fact, it is so beautiful that we cannot hold the experience of it for any length of time. We do not do it very often. The seventh level consists of a very few entities who, from the very beginning, have chosen to go back into the Uncreated Mass permanently—to go behind the Godhead. In no way does this take any power from God. In this way, we can face the divine without getting the full force of the Creator. In the first place, He cannot hold His force in a form for very long, and we cannot stay in His presence for too long. It is absolutely overwhelming, to the point that we feel as if we would burst. It is a wondrous feeling, but it is so full of love, exultation, and epiphany that we cannot hold it.

One of the greatest and highest avocations—to which I may someday try to aspire—is to be able to usher people back into the Godhead who do want to be there. It is very much like being there, but not—still keeping your individuality, but being right on the brink of the Godhead. Certain entities, when they are utterly advanced, choose to merge back with God. This is different from dark entities returning to the Godhead.

When we go into the seventh and draw the curtain behind us, we see before us a gigantic mosaic of wondrous faces. You might think it would be ugly, all those faces looking out at you, but it is not. It is absolutely beautiful. When the faces speak back, it sounds like something you would absolutely never begin to understand. The voices are also similar to something in the Akashic Records: the choruses that used to sing in Greece. I think that is where a lot of the theologians came up with the idea that angels sing, because of the beautiful tonal quality that comes out of the seventh. It is the most marvelous phenomenon; I thrill when I even think about it, for it has been far too long since I have been there.

There is a week of purification before we can go behind the seventh. We do not speak to anyone, but only walk around with a silver mantle over our face that means we are in meditative silence, waiting to go in. The men wear very silvery monk-cloth down over their faces, and the women wear veils. When we go in, we almost feel like brides or bridegrooms. Of course, now that I am a communicating spirit guide, I do not get to go so much because I am on call. When I used to lift my veil and go in, it was the most exalted feeling—immediately the voices seem to know what you feel, what is bothering you, what you would like to talk about, and the solution to what is of concern. Great knowledge and great benefit is derived from this. It is truly our tabernacle of sanctity.

Can we access the seventh level?

You can, but you will not feel the full impact, which would blow your physical body apart. You could certainly access it, but you must be taken there by two Archetypes, who stand at attention right before the curtain or veil across the entrance to the seventh. Now when you go, in your meditative practices, you must ask for two Archetypes to guide you.

Now I am going to tell you something very strange. Despite all the eons of time that I have lived in these quadrants, I, like you, am not from this planet. Of course I reside on its Other Side. We have to. When you have loved ones, you will still stay around and be a guide to those entities, not leaving them down in this awful place without protection.

We do not know where the seventh exists! We cannot find it. All we know is when we have kept our silver veil on and are ready to go, two Archetypes appear on either side of us. Then a curtain suddenly appears before us. It is not in any physical place, whereas the Hall of Wisdom, of course, is. I could tell you exactly what degree it is into the second quadrant, and exactly how many feet up it is. I could tell you where the park fountains are. We all know where everything is. Yet there is no "place" where the seventh exists. So we have surmised that it appears when it is needed. It is almost in another dimension, which leads us to believe and surmise that there are multiple dimensions that are still to be uncovered. You are all researchers, the same as I.

Can those who return to the Godhead ever come out?

Never! Only a few entities have ever been picked to go back. Sylvia has only known one in her whole lifetime. I have never known an entity that finally went behind the seventh and ever reemerged. Very, very few do this. It is almost nonexistent.

Most entities want to keep their individuality. I do not quite understand it, but some entities just want to return to God, which shows you the individuality of all Creation. Hundreds of them return to the seventh, but out of the ten billion on the Other Side, this is a very small percentage.

If they choose to return, they keep an identification of themselves. There is still individuality. When you visit behind the seventh, you see a myriad of distinctive faces. They do not have the merging, the living quarters, the research, or the mobility that we have. They are not able to walk around, love, have soulmates, or travel.

The Seven Lower Levels of Creation

In addition to the seven schematics of creation and the seven levels of the Other Side, there are seven lower levels of creation, which are quite fascinating. These are where all human thoughts reside that sometimes invade your dreamlike states—the monsters and grotesque things that come. These lower cultures live directly below this one. I do not want to say that all subconscious knowledge is stored there, but subconscious emanations tend to collect there.

Please recall that the seven levels of the Other Side ascend above us so that the first level is closest to us and the seventh is highest and farthest away. The lower levels of creation are in the opposite order: The first is highest—the closest to us—and the seventh is lowest. Level one is where wonderful sprites, fairies, elves, leprechauns, and gnomes reside. They are really a subculture. In this country, if you start talking about them, you will run into people who think you are really crazy. But you cannot tell anybody in the British Isles or the more Celtic countries that they do not exist. They do believe in what they call the little people—beautiful fairies and leprechauns.

Lilith governs this level. It is terrible that she has been portrayed as a witch. She was touted as the Queen of the Witches, which was another ignorance. They took a beautiful thing—her being Queen of the Fairies, and of the underworld, so to speak—and distorted it, saying that she was the woman of darkness. She is not! She is very close to Azna. She is a beautiful, wonderful entity, and she rules the first level, the domain of the little people.

Lilith lives in the underworld, which is a beautiful place, almost a fairyland. I know that she has had a life span now of 4,500 years. So they have a strange rejuvenation process.

Visually, the only thing that I can liken her to is a picture printed on the label of a Canadian soft drink that Sylvia once pointed out to me, of a fairy princess sitting on a leaf of some kind. This is how Lilith looks.

They do come to our Other Side, at least those on the first level do, but they do not need to. They can stay on Earth's plane for as long as the planet lasts, then eventually join with us. They do not have the adversity to overcome that you do. You see, they do not have a schematic of perfection. They are very much like animals—perfect in their own origins, without greed or such things to overcome. They live in an almost perfect environment.

What other creations occupy the first level?

This realm contains gnomes, fairies, elves, unicorns, dragons, Pegasus, mermaids, banshees, leprechauns, the Loch Ness monster, Big Foot, and all manner of human thought creations. Do you suppose that humans, even in their wildest imaginings, could have created these things if they were not infused with knowledge?

You might think I am given to fits of fantasy—but honestly, beautiful dragons live in this realm. I saw a golden-leafed one the other day that was absolutely beautiful. Within the first three lower levels, we even have magicians—the wonderful ones who created magic throughout the world. There is such a level of true magic and beauty. Look at some of your ancient Oriental art, how they used the gorgeous dragons as symbols of good. Those were all brought up from these beautiful lower levels.

Even the four lowest levels are not all that bad, but those levels are where the "waste" goes, the mental trash from our minds. Nothing in God's time or space is wasted anywhere. At the lowest level is where horrifying things exist. That is never tapped, unless it comes out in your nightmares. Please do not be concerned that these lower level horrors are evil or that they could ascend to your level. Almost all entities are kept within their levels. When you get to my side, you can visit any of these lower-level dominions. They are very interesting, not frightening. The Australian Aborigines are aware of all the devas of the plains. The Irish are aware of the leprechauns, and so on. Every culture has them.

Can Lilith help us in life?

Oh, yes. Absolutely. You can call upon her. The Fairy Queen is absolutely magnificent. She goes about the world doing wondrous good deeds. Her main focus is to take care of children. She has been in a terrible mess because there are so many missing children.

Unlike spirit guides, Lilith is the only one on her level—the highest on that side—who can cross dimensions. Once in a while, people will see the little people more than they will see spirits, because they are on a close vibrational level. In some countries, people will literally leave food out for these little people, who will come and take it. But those terrible stories about fairies stealing your baby are not true. No! Some countries have a custom of not telling the baby it is beautiful, because someone will hear it and steal it, or the "evil eye" will get the baby—that is not true.

When you go to bed at night, there are so many marvelous forces in the world you can call on. I always feel so sorry for those whom my voice cannot reach to tell them of the marvelous forces from God that are directly there to help them. Lilith is very good. Please, when you are dealing with a child of any age who might be in trouble, appeal to Lilith because she is the caretaker, the Beloved One of Children. She could almost be called a patron saint, as it were.

So remember, her name is Lilith. She is very powerful! The only one that we know of who really converses with Lilith is Azna. I myself have known Sylvia to speak to her. Sylvia did get hold of Lilith at one point in her life, but being so reasonable, she dropped it.

What is Lilith's purpose?

Protection. The tragedy is that you have so much protection around you and you have never known that you could call on it. It's as if somebody dropped you with your silver cord and your brain's little silver sparklers going off, but nobody gave you any maps of where the gullies and dark forests were, or where you would run into trolls. That's the worst part about life: You were thrown into a foxhole, and they made your radio go dead. Every time you stuck your head out, you got shot at.

All kinds of entities and devas are part of the molecular structure of the whole world—it is made up of entities and Archetypes that you can call on. You could have a fortress around you that nothing could penetrate!

How do these entities protect us?

They create a pushing effect. For example, when Sylvia investigated Sarah Winchester's house in San Jose, California, she was going to do a séance. They put her outside because she said, "I do not want to know anything that is going on. Set up the séance room; then I will come in." She was put out into the courtyard—but no one realized that a door automatically opened, and a giant German shepherd attack dog was let loose in the courtyard.

Sylvia was sitting on the bench and happened to look across the courtyard, and there was the dog standing perhaps 150 yards from her. Many animals are really not that sharp-sighted until they get close to you. They sense and sniff the air. This dog was very dangerous and weighed about 120 pounds. Sylvia was with someone at the time and said, "Do not move." She called me. I was frantic because I was not on a low enough level to get to that animal.

What I did was to call Lilith, who was on the same level. To this day, Sylvia thinks I did it. This is the first time in these 12 years that she will know I did not rescue her. "Francine," Sylvia said, "get that dog away from me, please." Instead, I got Lilith, who grabbed that dog by the scruff of the neck and pulled him away; then Sylvia ran inside. She said, "Francine, thank you so much. Thank you so much." But I did not do it! It was very frightening.

You ought to do the same if you are in a position like that. Please call on devas or lower-level entities to protect you. Especially if you came across a mother bear with her cubs. There is no way you could call your guide. We might not be able to help you. The Archetypes could probably push it off for a while, but you really want to call an entity on the same level.

So you see, there are levels of protection for you all over the place. Why would they not just know you are in trouble? Because they do not have a network to know every single human being who is in trouble. But by knowing their name, you can call them and an electrical current will be sent right to them like an alarm system, and they will know they are needed. They are not God—neither are we— and so cannot always keep everyone in their focus. So it is marvelous to say, "Lilith, please, attend me now!" Tell your guide to get Lilith. However, when you say her name, it has more impact, because you are closer to her level. But Sylvia did not know to call her, so I did. If you say her name, it also works wonderfully well with an ill animal. She is sort of the St. Francis of the lower level, and she protects animals. So if you have a cat or dog who needs protection or is sick, I would call on Lilith to attend.

Do the entities on the lower levels have bodies?

Yes. They sleep, eat, and procreate. But they live in an environment that is almost totally devoid of greed. When you get a culture that is devoid of greed, you have a perfect environment.

Do they reincarnate or change species?

No. They keep their phylum perfect. Lilith will always stay the way she is. She will never advance to a human level, but she is an entity directly from God that belongs to His own special creations.

Why does Lilith know about us?

Their life form is simpler. That is why an animal can spot a spirit faster than a human can. Have you ever watched a cat or dog bristle at something in a room and had no idea why? It's because their eyes are unclouded! The simpler life forms will know a tornado or earth-quake is coming long before you will, because of the innocence of their level. Animals do not need to perfect, so their minds are simply sensate, saying, "I need to eat. I need to sleep. I need to procreate." Higher levels, such as the sprites, do have sensate, thinking minds. But they do not have pain, remorse, guilt, or such things. They are good. They, as well as the devas, are constantly attending to humanity.

Can we appeal to Lilith for lost animals?

Yes, because Lilith has been known to bring animals back. Ask Lilith to solve that for you. You might be very surprised at how powerful she is.

Why would Lilith care about us?

Lilith really has great power. She has actually been called Cupid, as well as the Messenger, which was attributed to Mercury, the god with wings on his feet. But she is also a message carrier. Those are all attributed to her.

Lilith is very advanced; she can trilocate. She is almost the Goddess of her world and domain. She has great lateral movement and great power. If she cannot be there, then she can send her consorts. Just as Azna has a multiplicity and is like a sparkler that shoots out all over, so is Lilith for her level. You might be very surprised at the fact that Father God, or the male counterpart of God, cannot do that. He cannot move! But by His very hand, He holds everything stable. She is the other hand that moves.

Are there "little green men"?

No. If you see them, you are in a drug-induced state, and the mind is conjuring up parts of things and putting them together, especially from the subconscious, which fragments reality in dreams. You may combine the nose of an aardvark and the feet of a duck, or see a pink elephant. We do not know of any pink elephants. What happens is the mind fragments many images and does an overlay, creating grotesqueness. That is how monsters are created. Such thought creations go to the lowest levels.

The Levels of Discarded Thoughts

The second level is very peculiar and has to do with all thoughts that are accumulated. It is a nebulous place, their equivalent of our Akashic Records. I find it to be thick and frightening. It is not evil, but it roars. It is terrible. Can you imagine if you went into someone else's mind, what you would hear? That is what I find it to be.

I do know spirit guides—not to be egotistical, but they are not as advanced—who have a great time on the second level; they go down and pick out thoughts. I do not like it at all. Maybe this is a weakness on my part, but I do not like that much noise. I did not like the few times that Sylvia has gone to places where there is loud music, either. I think the reason my ears have been so sensitized, as with most guides, is because we have to listen for you. The longer you are in life, the more sensitive we become. I remember that before I was a guide to Sylvia, I could go to these places and sort of wander around. I cannot go anymore.

The entities that have been brave enough to go have said there are beautiful places, but I do not trust it. It gets beautiful, and then it gets ugly real fast. You can never guess what thought might jump out at you, literally. You know how you have to govern your own mind in order to keep your thoughts intact? Imagine being in a giant one in which you are at the mercy of any thought that hits you.

Do all thoughts go to this level?

Yes. Every thought that has ever been. It is scary. I think if anybody wanted to have a hell, that would be it. I contend that at times, certain people who went there thought it was hell. There is weeping, wailing, hysterical laughing, thoughts, moans, and feelings. It is just hideous! It is terribly sensual. Dante must have visited these different levels. I really recommend Dante's *Inferno,* not that I necessarily want you to get into classical reading. He talks about the different levels of hell. It is a very interesting story, is it not? How people have food and they cannot eat; they want sex and cannot have it, and on and on it goes. It is very much like that thick level. We do not know for sure, but possibly people created this from drunkenness and drug addiction.

Thoughts are things—and this is where those thoughts reside. Where do you go but where your thoughts take you? It is not a reality, but it becomes one. Nobody ever stays there for very long. You cannot get caught in there. But I do think that people go down sometimes to this terrible level, and because of the thought-forms that take shape, are convinced that this is where hell is. Of course, if they think it is, what happens? Right at that moment, the thought becomes a thing. So they have a green monster or a red-tailed demon with a fork. They've got it all.

Religious fanatics also dip into that nightmare level. The biggest fanatics are those who are always preaching about hellfire and brimstone. Their thoughts become things, and they begin to create their own demons. They bring these awful, ugly, horrible things into their minds. So what they are doing is possessing themselves by their own thoughts.

Nightmares are from the second level?

Yes, some nightmares seep up from the second level. Now, the guardian of that level is Lilith. She can cement it closed. If you are having trouble with nightmares, you can certainly petition Lilith to close that "door." You do not have to keep dipping down to that level. As people become more entrenched in the physical level of Earth and become more negative, they get closer to this level where "thoughts are things."

Levels four through seven are really the mind refuse. Level one has all the beauty that existed. Levels two and three are almost cemented together. Then the four lower levels are the mental mind dumps. Sometimes I think they leak back and forth, but they do not get up to the first level because that is Lilith's domain. Now, are they ever let out? No! The only way they can ever be accessed is from your own mind.

The lower levels, from three on down, are very monsterlike. Not only do they have stored knowledge of pterodactyls and dinosaurs and all the other things that have existed, but they also have all the ugliness that has been created out of the subconsciousness of humankind. It is a nightmare world, very much like what the ancients believed was the underworld. This is where the idea of "hell" came from, because of all those demonic, ugly things.

What is amazing, too, is that the sky is very dark in the lower levels. Above me, when I went in there, it was like an electrical storm going on all the time. I felt like I was in a giant brain, and it was very frightening. Very few things frighten me. If there is any "hell," that is where it resides. But no entity resides there. We have never lost an entity. Not even the dark entities like to go there, so you can imagine that it is very unpleasant.

It is nice that the levels do not leak over to each other, but the horror is that people can transfer their thoughts to others. Many times in the sleep state, you will absorb someone else's thought manifestation; it will come to you as a nightmare, and it's almost like being psychically attacked in your sleep. They cannot hurt you, but I am sure that everyone has had one of those nights where they have sat bolt upright in bed, sweating profusely because one of these thought-forms has invaded their sleep state. There again, the innocence of the sleep state gives rise to that. Children are more prone to viewing these strange life-forms.

In near-death experiences, some people see a "hell."

Absolutely. They got down into the lower levels. No entity in a physiological state should try to go there. It would not hurt you, but you would only go once.

Ask Lilith to close the door so you do not slip into that level. That is why children will have nightmares. Children are such marvelously advanced entities. They really do not want to be in their bodies. They are always out skipping around. Sylvia's son Christopher almost drove us crazy. He was always on the steps of the Hall of Wisdom. I must have chased him away at least four or five times a week. That is also frightening, because a child can slip and go into these other levels. They start playing with the fairies. This is why I say, stay on your own level! It is wonderful to believe in fairies and know they are there, as well as the beautiful unicorns and all that, but stay on your own level.

Our thoughts are mostly unusable creations?

That is right. However, Tibetan masters can create an entity of pure thought energy called a tulpa, which can actually sustain a type of life for a short time. I do not think the lowest four levels of the nightmare realm are important, except for the simple fact that you know they exist. The first level is an actual creation, but the other six are made of thought-things. They are creations of ours. Lilith and the fairies are actual creations of God.

It goes to show you that humanity, as great as it is, and even though it is part of God, does not create many good things. Lots of evil things are created, but they are relegated to this lower under-world from which they cannot escape. The only way they escape is through thought processes. They are not really there. It is brought through by hallucination. No ugly creature from the lower level is going to come and bite your leg tonight. There is no such thing.

ॐ ॐ ॐ

Out of my night torn with a black pitiless rage,
my lark of sunlight and faith seemed shattered in the wind.

It seemed to fall silently into the sea, never to rise again.
But then where shall morning wander without the lark's heralding
cry? Without faith, will it lock its shafts of light in a vault and die?

— Sylvia

ॐ ॐ ॐ ॐ ॐ ॐ

Part III

TOOLS FOR LIFE

Chapter 12

TRANSFORMING NEGATIVE ENERGY

Francine: I want to talk to you about energy. I know that there has been so much talk about negative energy, especially with the spirituality movement coming into its own. I want you to know that all energy is positive. I want you to quit speaking in terms of negative energy, because that gives dark forces a channel into you.

All energy is good. It changes depending on what you do with it. The birth of energy is all good, because it is neutral. Neutral energy is simply benign and good.

If you give energy to something that is negative—such as worry, anxiety, or fear—then you build it to such a state that it becomes worse than any action directed toward you. Let us say you have a problem with death. That in itself is not a negative phenomenon. Death, as we know it, is a positive transformation. It is very much like being on an island from which you are finally rescued. This Earth is like an island of thorns and problems, then all of a sudden, a wonderful silver UFO comes down and takes you to the Other Side, which is where you belong in the first place. You are only transplanted here for a few years—even if it is 80 or 90—to see how well you can survive.

Most cultures, especially those that you call primitive, look at death as being a journey to a greater place, a happiness. The ancient Mesopotamians, the early Greeks, the Sumerians, and every one of the ancient cultures, as well as the Third World cultures—all look at it as a release. Even warriors killed in battle in American Indian cultures were seen as victorious, because they conquered life.

In your culture, you are constantly trying to ward off aging and death. You are constantly bombarded on the small boxes that you watch—I believe you call this TV—with information about making yourself not age and forestalling the Grim Reaper. There is goodness in this message, as everyone wants to stay well and keep their bodies in shape as long as they are here. No one wants their house to be in disrepair, yet do not be *obsessed* with aging and death. Too many people look at death as being an evil of sorts—not you who are spiritually advanced, but most people. When you are around those people who direct this kind of emotion toward you, you can absorb this negative energy, if you are not prepared. Because you are sensitive, it will become part of you for a while until you learn to cleanse it.

Begin by addressing the fact that you are a spiritual entity with nothing but neutral and positive energy; I guarantee you that you will not have the problems that you had before. Be aware of how energy is directed toward you and what people say to you. Make yourself like a funnel or a sieve. If a person gets mad at you for no reason and starts offending you, then say to yourself—mentally, if not directly to the person—"I do not accept your anger, rage, or hostility." Feel as if it is beautiful, clear water running through a sieve. You have purified and neutralized the energy sent to you. You have done a very beautiful thing: Now that you have neutralized that negative energy; it cannot harm anyone.

You have to say, in all truthfulness, "Give it your best shot!" Instead of resisting, try to just relax and let it pass through. If you do, it goes away. The harder you fight, the more negativity you add to it. They really cannot do much beyond scaring you. Let them do whatever they wish. Trust me when I tell you that it will subside.

When you get a harsh note from someone, when there is bad news, or when you get something that gives you anxiety, take a deep breath and say, "I will not let this impact me. It cannot affect me. I am like a sieve through which water just simply runs. It cannot stick or cling to me; I will not give any voice, knowledge, or reality to it!"

If you are having money or financial problems or a lawsuit, and you are distraught, then petition Azna. Mother God will interfere and help you with this. She can use Her beautiful golden sword to transform this negative energy.

You should not send negative energy back to its source. If you pull from that negative energy and slap back, do you know what happens? It begins to spiral. Now sometimes, you must fight fire with fire, because occasionally negative energy rises in such a flame that you must rage out against it. But when you do, I want you to think of it as a pure flame that burns hot blue—a pure fire. If somebody is out to get you or you feel threatened, immediately begin to purify that negative energy. If you start doing that, it will be as automatic to you as breathing or blinking an eye. It should be, so you are not attacked. You have at your disposal every defense against anyone that is out to hurt or harm you. If you are concerned about your job, loved ones, family, or people around you that are hurt, then you can surround them with a blue flame as well as white light, because that will burn out a lot of your illnesses. If someone is sick, think of them as surrounded by tons of blue flame. If you have a problem of infertility, think of your organs as being cleansed by this blue flame. You can use green, too, but think about how powerful the blue flame is. Very hot!

Now what about a righteous, justifiable fight? Is that negative? Whatever starts from a pure motive is also pure energy. Many crusades that you take up have a positive bearing and positive energy. People say, "I put out positive energy, but I get back nothing but negativity." Well, for every positive bit of energy that rises, so does the negative rise with it. Because God is love and goodness—I know it is hard to see, but it is always true—the positive outweighs the negative. It does! The ultimate is that you have the last laugh, because you eventually come to the Other Side, and that is the positive balance.

How can we stop verbal abuse?

It would be so much better to light a white candle, open up your hands, pray, and surround the person with white light. If you really want to stop verbal abuse, then put a purple light around their mouth. Not so much to bind their mouths, but to give them judgment. To open up their God-Center so that they see what is just and what is right. I would much prefer that you petition God to allow them to see the light, rather than do anything to them: Let them be opened to what is truth. You will ask that the person, from that point on, would just speak spiritual truth. The purple light is the highest of spiritual colors. Say, "When speaking to me, about me, or for me, this person can only speak spiritual truth."

Spells and Magic

In themselves, spells carry with them so much negativity, because they have been used since ancient times for ill. Yet the ancient shamans used them primarily for healing. Dolls were cast to make health come about, which is imitative magic—so is lighting a candle, or the marvelous method of taking a loved one's picture and holding a green light on it. These are all great examples of positive, shaman-istic, imitative magic.

However, when you get into St. Joan's root and dragon's blood, you start calling on ancient rituals—which are not bad in themselves, but they have been used negatively for so long. For the same reason, we never use red or black candles because they are used for malig-nant rituals. The candles in themselves are not bad. Similarly, I would not want you to hang a crucifix upside down—not because the cruci-fix has any power, but only because it has symbolized positive ener-gy, and if you abort it into its opposite, it then becomes negative. Often, people who are spiritual go into many things, trying to find out where the power source is, but finally, they realize that it is within their God-Center and that they do not need any of that paraphernalia.

The shamans and early Wiccans practiced and believed in imitative magic. I have never addressed this because it gets out of hand too easily. Any ritual that you do is imitative magic. *Magic* is a crude word to use because it sounds like you are doing something that is above God's law, but really you are not. I am not ever in favor of making dolls that represent people. I think that is idolatry.

What is Wicca?

Since ancient times, Wiccans have believed in the energy and power of the forces of nature. In the early days, Wiccans believed in the Mother God. Women of the Wiccans were revered as healers and prophets. In the patriarchal religions, men were revered and women denigrated because they bled and were thought to be unclean. That was terrible for women and is still practiced today.

Wicca is a spiritual belief that the Mother Goddess rules the planet and is to be revered because She gave birth to the planet—and in actuality, She did! The living planet is Her domain; She also has other planets to which She concurrently attends.

People have always had a problem with the Mother Goddess concept because it has belonged to the nature religions, who have always believed in Her. The word *witch* came from *Wicca,* so it has always had a bad connotation—as you know, during the Dark Ages innocent herbalists and healers were often put to death as "witches."

I think there are good Wiccans, but I think anyone who professes to be a witch has to be very careful, because that title in itself carries with it a dark and ominous meaning. It is a power trip, and people have to be very wary. Besides, it has nothing to do with Gnostic Christianity.

Do rituals have any power?

I think you are always going to have people who think that. I think that is what has happened in religions for years. The ritual itself became the focus, to the point that people did not know why things were in chalices, had crucifixes on them, or were covered with purple—and furthermore, they did not care. There is no power to a candle, except that which we give to it.

Here is an example of imitative magic: Let us say a woman decides that she is going to go outside on a beautiful moonlit night, and the wind is blowing in her face, and she picks up a handful of earth, mixes it with water, and sprinkles it in a circle around her. She says, "By the forces of nature and God, I wish to be protected."

This is wonderful—not because it calls upon on any forces, but because you are allowing yourself to be part of the forces. This is what the great shamans talked about. You should not draw a picture of someone and bind their mouth; I do not like that, because it seems as if you are sending something bad to that person. The visualizations I will soon discuss are just as powerful. Making up your own shamanistic rituals is beautiful, because it is using all the powers of fire, water, earth, and air to call upon the energies of God. But to start making figures—I am not saying it is wrong, I just do not give any credence or belief to it.

Totems

Know what a totem is? Sylvia's totem is an elephant. In other words, it is a spirit of nature. The American Indians know this better than anyone; they have always been *shamanistic,* which means "of the earth, where all of nature is sacred." No other culture has had it so clearly and so beautifully as they have. They adopted an animal such as a wolf, cougar, or eagle for protection. Stop and think in your own mind, *What is your favorite animal?* That animal will be your totem. I would not necessarily pick a mouse to protect you.

Not very long ago, an amazing thing happened. Sylvia's husband, Larry, has a black panther totem. It is quite large. One of their neighbors walked by their window one day and said, "I could not believe it. There was a huge black cat sitting in the window." It was Larry's totem. I am sure they would have died had they seen an elephant in the front room!

So regardless of what it is, pick an animal that also represents how you feel about yourself. The elephant is sturdy and faithful; it plods along, never giving up—it is stubborn. That is Sylvia's totem. So think about what yours is. What you adopt at this point will be the thing that protects you.

Can we merge with animals?

Yes, absolutely! You can merge with anything you want. You can even merge your soul with a cheetah and run like the wind, or merge your soul with a bird and fly. That is what the American Indians did. They believed that you could merge with animals. It is also where the pantheistic movement came from. Pantheism is the belief that God is in everything—in every tree and boulder, every dwelling and device, in parts of plants, ceiling beams, a candle. This belief is very ancient for humanity. However, it is mixed up. Could we not experience the plant? Of course, but God is not the plant. It is an offshoot of what God made. The very same as a child is an offshoot of the parental figure in life. But they are not the parent.

ॐ   ॐ   ॐ

Dear God,

I know I speak across timeless years and lives,
and I know that You have been with me no matter
what path I have taken.

I also see You lovingly before me, watching with patient eyes;
each tear I've shed is only in the space of Your heartbeat.

Hope springs within me that each laugh and tear lights a path to You;
to be is only to exist in loving You and in You loving me.

In this, I have acquired not only the hope,
but the belief in my immortality.

— Sylvia

ॐ ॐ ॐ ॐ ॐ ॐ

Chapter 13

LIGHTS AND COLORS

Raheim: Lights are very important to your well-being and health. Try wearing different colors, and watch how people respond to you. If you wear certain colors, people will immediately come up to you and start responding. Clergy and such people have worn white and black for many years. This causes the most benign inner reactions with people. Also, people in black are far more approachable because there is no color to reflect. That does not mean I want you to wear black always, but I am saying that if you are going on an interview or something in which you want people to respond to you, then wear black, and possibly gray and maroon. Those are the primary colors for optimum success. If you are going to a job or situation that has to do with animals, flowers, or plants, then wear green.

Francine: When you are in a dull mood, everyone says to wear bright colors. I agree with that to a certain extent. But there is nothing that beats black and white, or just black, because black is a combination of everything. If you take a palate of color and mix it all together, do you know what you will get? Black. Many people think that wearing so much black means you are somber or dark. No! It does not mean that. Black has always been the humility color. That is why ministers down through the ages have been asked to wear black.

In the absence of color, all color is available.

There is something so pristine about black. I myself, on my side, wear black most of the time. If you get very, very astute, you can almost tell what people on my side are working on by the colors they seem to fancy.

However, when you are feeling down, try to wear something gold or purple. When really in doubt, wear black. You do not want to wear too much blue unless you want to put yourself into a blue frame of mind, literally. Blue is the lofty color. Green, aquamarine, and such colors are very growing and alive.

Raheim: The one color that people do not respond to, I will tell you, is the color red, which stimulates passion and the adrenal glands. Now, in wintertime wearing red is very good, especially if you wear it in nightwear, because it stimulates circulation. The color red really does not exist on our side except in roses and hues of pale mauve. There are peaches, pinks, what we call "cherry-blossom" flavoring, melon, and offshoots of the color rose or the more orange colors; however, there are no real reds, because that stimulates passion and anger.

Still, if you find that people say you look wonderful in red, then this could possibly be your color, and you should wear it. But I will tell you to wear it sparingly. We see more people in accidents and having problems with red cars, clothing, or anything red. Accidents will occur more rapidly with the color red. Red will create aggravated people around you.

Stones

Amethyst is universally the best color of crystal for everyone. Here we go back to the purple. If you are not going to do that, then get a white quartz. White or even pink quartz, by the way, is very good, because pink brings about love. Both white and purple are for protection. An amethyst brings about healing and rejuvenation.

What about silver-looking stones?

They are beautiful, but I would not use any of the smoky, dark colors. But if you start getting into the darker tourmaline colors, those are not positive. I do not think that you want to use anything "smoky" other than citron, because that is more gold or orange. Dark topaz is not good because then you are into the smoky quartz. Tiger's eye is good, because of course it has yellow and gold tones, which are very good.

Your Aura

The world is becoming so complex that the more you can simplify, the better. Do you know that your aura can be in direct discord with the colors you are wearing, and that this can actually weaken it? If you wear too much color or are too gaudy, your aura flames out on it. When you dress, think about your aura colors. However, be very skeptical of these silly aura pictures you can get at carnivals and fairs. Everybody looks the same. It is just a refraction of light.

Your aura is nothing more than an electrical emanation—a halo around you, the same as the saints were painted with halos. Everyone has rainbow colors in their aura. When you are dressing in the morning, think about which color you would like to emanate for that day. White gives off light and is closest to the body. It is the color that comes from our God, the Holy Spirit. The rest of the colors do not emanate in this way. Gold often bands white; it does not give off a shaft of light, but it is iridescent. Purple then bands the gold. When you are concentrating very spiritually, purple comes. Purple is probably the most dominant color of spirituality. So we have white, gold, and purple. Emerald-green bands that, and from there we get the "variables"—shades of yellow and pink. We do not get red in the aura unless the person is ferociously mad. If the person is sick, we get black. If they are in a mood, we get muddy colors. Blue is wondrous but icy. Most people think blue is very warm, but it is cold. So is green. Orange is warm.

Are white, gold, and purple always around us?

They are the primary bands, yes. The derivatives—yellow, pink, green, and the rest—are far more into the female spectrum. Emotion has more bands of color added on. This is almost a signal to us that you are becoming much more emotional. Women add new bands of color through life, but men do not, unless their emotions become highly developed, which happens very rarely.

White, gold, and purple surround you unless there is illness or death. Then the whole thing will turn dark and muddy, as it will if there is an evil entity present or if the ego is out of whack. If the ego goes out of whack, it has to do with cruelty, meanness, avarice, or bossiness. Stupidity is another good one—that is an evil in itself. You must know that. No one has the right to be stupid, unless of course there is some congenital retardation. But to walk around in the world and be stupid—*that* is stupid! There is no excuse to be either stupid or mean. Every thought and feeling that you have flits across your aura, and we see it. Now you may think that this violates your privacy. We cannot necessarily read the thoughts, but we certainly know what mood you are in by what your aura range is.

The amazing thing is that when you walk into a room, any negative energy you may have can shoot out as far as 200 feet. However, even the most positive energy you can have will only shoot out 30 to 40 feet. This is because this world is not conducive to positive energy; it gets trapped and blocked. When you walk into a room, be aware and try hard; ask that your energy be spread out at least 30 feet. Think of it expanding and breathing as a living thing; think of it bathing the room. Maybe you can get it to 50 feet, but it cannot go 200 feet. That is why you will spot negativity faster than positive energy. Positivity does not go that far, because this Earth, of course, is not conducive to it: You will feel it in offices, group settings, parties, concerts—you can just feel it.

We are so worried about white-lighting ourselves. That is fine, too, but you should bathe the room in gold. Do not be so closed in, because negativity—one negative person—can infect a group far more than a jolly person can have any effect.

Here is an amazing thing: If a person is on stage, for instance, and exuding positive energy, then other positive energy reaches up to meet it. But negative energy would not; that keeps to itself. But when your positive energy reaches others, that energy gains in momentum. So you are adding 30 feet to 30 feet to 30 feet to 30 feet. It is so marvelous to collect positive energy because it spreads and beats negative energy.

When a room is filled with positive energy, it is bright, with a rose and golden tinge. When it is filled with negativity, it looks like cheesecloth, hazy and murky green. It has a texture and a sickness to it. By negativity, I do not mean suffering, and I do not mean death. These are parts of life. I mean someone who is evil or bad or psychically not in tune with their own spirit, or who is too involved with their own ego. Do not tell me that you have not been in a situation in which you felt the air thicken on you, or you felt that you could not breathe or the energy was thick and stifling. It has nothing to do with whether the room is hot. Whenever you start getting sick to your stomach and you do not have the flu, chances are that your solar plexus is reacting to negativity. If you get a headache right away and you have no sinus problems, your body is reacting biologically to negativity.

Can we speed up our spiritual lessons?

Oh yes, yes. Ask that your lessons be condensed so that you get through them faster. You can do that. You see, you are not blocking your own free will. Think about this: Do you want childbirth to go on for 38 hours or only 2? Do you want to have the flu for 30 minutes or 24 hours? You can learn just as much in 30 minutes. People do not know they have the right to say that. They linger for three years before they die, although anyone can speed that up just through their will.

How can we battle ignorance?

You must learn, be together, and spread the light. That is why Novus Spiritus is so important. I am probably more dedicated to getting people in than Francine. She is much more soft-peddled than I am. I don't mean you won't be "saved" without going to church, but in a spiritual gathering place, you will certainly find that your soul is worth saving. Each person, each light that you bring in, brings up your light until it becomes a magnificent spectrum, a huge monolith of light. That is the only reason to do it—not because you want a lot of money or members, although money would be nice to build a church, but that is not the primary thing. It is to increase spirituality. It has always been that way.

Anyone who wants to be a minister, or to administer to people, will do so. There is no doubt about that. You are right on the brink, as Francine says, "of the greatest epiphany you will ever see." *Epiphany* means "a rebirth of religious belief as it should be." Every one of you is a warrior of light, fighting against darkness. You bet!

Can a very negative person still be very psychic?

No, anyone who is negative cannot stay psychic.

As our light gets brighter, do we attract more people?

Oh, of course. That is part of it. Then as people come to you, you must keep pushing them back on themselves so that they will gain their own strength and answers. Many people who come to Sylvia must be constantly put back on themselves. Otherwise, any leader gets their ego out of whack, and an entourage of salivating people hanging around and licking your feet, which so many people with lesser souls want.

Unfortunately, as you attract light, you will also attract dark with it. So you are really fighting a war. But oh, what a wondrous thing! I feel so bad sometimes that I have not come into life at this wondrous time, because I am a warrior. I would have loved to have fought all these things. My time was about A.D. 750. It was not a fun time; it was very quiet, peaceful, and boring. I would have loved to fight—to put on my armor, go charging out, and slash through some darkness. I would have loved that. You do not know what an exquisite time you live in. Truly exquisite!

Do not listen to anyone who tells you that this is a negative time. Of course things are difficult in many ways, but it is a wondrous time to excel. It is probably the greatest time! Think about it: People say, "You cannot make Earth like the Other Side." Yes, you can! A little bit of heaven can be here if you have regular meetings where your worries are gone. That is the little bit of heaven that is acquired in this life!

You had a lifetime on Earth in A.D. 750?

Yes, only one lifetime. I am known as one of the patrons or protectorates over on this side, and that was given to me by God. So I have become the protectorate of mission life entities, which means I am always around. I was actually given the Sword from Azna to be the protectorate; I value that more than any physical life.

In my life, I was known as a guru. I was part of a group of people now known as *dervishes*. We, in our lifetime, did much as far as healing is concerned. I stand, in life and on the Other Side, approximately 5'11" in height, so you will know what I look like. I wear the type of turban of the Sikhs. I have a very dark complexion and very large eyes. My looks on the Other Side correlate very much with someone you may know by the name of Korla Pandit. People have been able to see me even more so than Francine, because my energy is stronger.

Your physical body is not yours. You are absolutely not in your body. The more you can absorb this fact, the healthier you will be. Your soul exists approximately five to six inches above your body. When you become laden in your body, you begin to have physical illness. I want you to start reiterating this daily: "I am *not* my body. I am above my body." Now, you do not want to be like some spiritual people and go into the state of nirvana in this life. No! You are reaching toward nirvana, but this is a passive state in which you are not able to do good works in the world.

Francine: The ancient yogis did not even want to be in the body, which is nonproductive. The true avatars begin to rise *above* their own bodies. At the other extreme, you find people who are very earthbound, very tied up in their own bodies. They get overly vain, overly conscientious, and overly self-conscious about themselves. That is really a type of spiritual death.

Synesthesia

Synesthesia is an ability that all of you have to feel sound and color. This is found in the limbic part of the brain, which is very near the hypothalamus. The limbic system is found in every animal. You also have it in your brain, but you do not use it. It is what they call the old, primordial brain. This primordial brain is where the animal in all human beings was sensate enough to begin to convert sounds and colors into words and symbols. You all did this in Atlantis, but you have forgotten it.

Synesthesia is different from synergism, which is the simple act of collectively putting together something out of nothing using the imagination. Synesthesia has always existed: It is where you begin to vibrate with certain sounds and convert them into colors and numbers. I am told by the master teachers that once this is brought to your consciousness, you will never again be able to not vibrate with this. In other words, the number six will always have a specific color attached to it. Someone's name will have a particular aroma and color attached to it.

You may feel that this seems very convoluted, but when you start asking your mind, "What color does that vibrate to?" you are going to be able to differentiate between dark, gray, and light entities. So when this limbic part of your brain is activated, you will always be able to determine if there is darkness in a human being.

I want you to begin to vibrate the colors. When you hear someone's name, I want you to say to yourself, "What color does this remind me of?" Now if there are two Debras in a room, get in the presence of one Debra and say to yourself, "What number does this person vibrate for me? Does she feel like a vibration of a number? A color?" Then go even further: "What aroma does she vibrate?"

Now, speaking of aroma, you have got to start designating your own scent. If you do not have one, absorb one. If you want to vibrate gardenia, jasmine, sandalwood, or rose, you do not have to get that scent from the store. You can vibrate any aroma that you desire.

Let us take the people you love. You know that your child, spouse, or lover has a particular smell. You know their odor, but you never take the next logical step. It is very much as if the mind's deductive reasoning has been taken away by civilization. You must start living more primordially in order to survive. Whether you believe it or not, you are living in a very dark, dank jungle. Just because there are flashy cars on the street, nice paint on the walls, and even running water doesn't mean you are not in a jungle! The jungle is getting thicker with beasts that run in the night who come in human form.

Synthesize vibrations. I want to show you how this operates: Stop now and think. Start by closing your eyes. I am going to mention certain things or objects to you: A bundt cake. The name Lily. Salt. Chalk.

Open your eyes. When I said "bundt cake," could you smell it? Could you see it? Did you get a golden brown or a frosting? Did you feel there was a number or something else attached to it? What number did you get? A four or a six would not be wrong. A bundt is round and stands on four; probably you could also say six. If you do not interpret it into numbers, that is all right—just try to vibrate the sound, smell, and color.

What about Lily? If you thought of a woman, you were vibrating right. But if you thought of a flower, you were not vibrating wrong. So much of this is culturally determined. Did you get a white flower? Did you get an aroma, texture, or a feel?

How about salt? Did you get the whiteness, the texture? It would be very advanced to get an overflow of salt, a lot of salt pouring. How about chalk? Did you get a smell from chalk? A feeling? That is what you want to do: Start feeling, sensing, smelling, and vibrating it; then the numbers will come.

What you want to do is start vibrating to the glowing ability of a person. What level of gold or dark or gray is transmitted by even their name and presence? You want to start realizing what numbers they are vibrating. Learn to sense the vibrations of dark entities. Odd numbers indicate that the person is in terrible straits; even numbers show much more stability. Anything that has to do with threes shows that they are elevated. If a person starts vibrating to you in nine, that is the highest spirituality. So this is another way to see whether a person is good, bad, or indifferent. See what number they are vibrating. Take your first inclination and also get a textural feel of them.

If you use this technique, you are really going to get a very clear picture of the person. As you ask for their aroma or color, each thing adds to the aura. That is what the truest aura is. You know that certain people have a distinct aroma. I come in on jasmine. Sylvia's grandmother comes in on lilac. Have you ever touched a baby's garment and known that entity? You say, "This smells like my baby." That is how animals have always distinguished who their young are, even among thousands of others. It is in the limbic part of the brain.

What do you mean by "vibrating"?

You think of it, feel it, sense it, and see what color it vibrates for you. You can really vibrate any number you wish. Try to start by vibrating a number divisible by three. It does not matter if all of you start vibrating nine. It would be wondrous! I like the three myself because I like the Trinity feeling. Five and seven, even though they have been called holy, are numbers of conflict because they have edges that have not been rounded off, so there is always an odd shoe left to drop. But rounded off is purposeful and going forward, because a wheel will roll faster than a square. So three, six, or nine are numbers you should vibrate.

Then begin to feel your own vibration of color. Decide what color you wish to vibrate, or what color is indigenous and natural to you. If you vibrate green all the time, that is wonderful because it is healing, both self-healing and outward healing. Sylvia's color is very mauve and pink.

Regardless of what your aura is doing, you are always vibrating the same color close to your body. Many aura readers mistakenly try to read the outward layers, which are nothing more than passing moods. The aura that stands about four inches from the body and hugs the body is the aura that is indigenous to everyone. What you can do is keep increasing your green, if that is your natural color, to make it more emerald, richer, deeper, darker, and brighter.

Does Sylvia sense her audiences?

Yes. She can taste the audience. She feels its vibration and senses it because the limbic part of her brain is very accelerated. I am trying to give you the ability to expand to this psychic position of tasting and feeling. As Sylvia has said, "You see babies, and you want to eat them. You want to put their feet in your mouth. You want to bite their little bottoms and chew their toes." There is something very edible about babies, or loved ones, though not in a real, literal sense. Watch animals in play: They will literally bite each other. We have gotten away from tasting, hugging, and smelling—the whole aromatic celebration of another human being.

ॐ ॐ ॐ

Society of Novus Spiritus's Daily Prayer

Dear Father and Mother God,

Surround me with:

A white light of the Holy Spirit,
A gold light of God-Centeredness,
A purple light of spirituality, and
A silver light of higher consciousness.

Cement my intellect to my emotion,
Release all negativity within, and
Keep all negativity from entering.

These things I ask in God's name.

ॐ ॐ ॐ ॐ ॐ ॐ

Chapter 14

Protection Against Psychic Attack

Francine: If your dreams are very strange and restless, it could be that a dark entity is psychically attacking you. If you have not felt it at night, then in the day you could have felt it—tiredness; unease, especially at night; malaise; strange dreams; and all the funny, spooky feelings that you get. That is all part of an attack. You find yourself short-tempered, cross, irritable, despairing, and moody. It takes a physiological toll, too. The body begins to feel a tiredness, because darkness saps energy. Now be thankful whenever that comes. That means good is rising beyond it. It is ridiculous in many ways to be happy about an attack, but it is comforting to know that everyone has experienced it.

Raheim: We see psychic attack as a clawing of the mind. If you experience the following symptoms, then you either have a chemical imbalance, or someone is psychically attacking you. Psychic attack has the following symptoms:

- feeling daily anxieties;
- feeling riddled with worries that are not akin to you;

- waking up with dread in the morning; and
- always having that half-feeling that something is wrong.

Can a psychic attack be directed against us?

A psychic attack can be directed *toward* you. For instance, a person who wants you for themselves and cannot have you can send you a negative attack, or perhaps someone who has jealousy toward you, some co-worker or family member. The person may be doing this knowingly or unknowingly. If you were to know how truly absorbent most human beings are psychically, then you might be fearful if you did not know the tools by which to fight it.

You know when you have been caught in a psychic attack because you feel as if something has suddenly enveloped you, strangling off your air and your wind. In this situation, all you have to do is ask for the white, gold, and purple band to be expanded. Everything in you knows how to do this. You can do it mentally.

There are many other forms of negativity besides psychic attack. For example, Sylvia once traveled through Pacheco Pass, a highway in California, and caught all kinds of horrible images. She was not being attacked; she simply happened to get into a stationary vortex of pain, horror, and accidents. But as soon as that place and time were behind her, so were those images.

What color is a psychic attack?

A very heavy, thick, green, murky-looking substance appears around the entity. It is almost a muddy chartreuse color that we see. So we know then that you are under attack.

Now, if the person is attacking themselves, which happens very frequently, the color turns brown, which means they are being self-centered and thinking, *I'm sorry for myself; I feel bad; I'm angry. Me, me, me.* You will notice that these people wear brown a lot.

Should I try to change negative people?

Francine: Absolutely. But make sure you wear your overcoat, so to speak. "Pump up your light and put it out"—this is a wonderful way to put it. You must always stay in the loop—you cannot run and hide from life. You have to be out there. But you certainly do not want to go out in a rainstorm without a raincoat on. That is stupid. All I want to do is give you the protection and still get out there.

Should we confront a psychic attacker?

Raheim: I would not call them on the phone, because a lot of times, when people are attacking, they are not even aware of it. Let us say you are being attacked by a co-worker in some department next to yours, and every time you walk by, they are sneering, and they do not like you. Why would you call that person on the phone—to be put on report as being a crazy person?

It is better to put up a mental shield—we call it the golden shield—and use the Sword of Azna to cut off the negative energy. You can find out who is attacking you by visualizing a blackboard in your mind and asking your guide to write the person's name on it. You will be surprised at how the name begins to appear. If you see it written on the blackboard, you have already named the person and it already begins to diminish.

Are curses real?

No. The curse is a phenomenon that is only effective if the intended victim believes in it. The negativity would be felt by you just the same as somebody sending you hate, jealousy, or unwanted love or desire. It really is no more important than that—even dolls with pins in them or wax figures that you burn up. I do not care if there are nail clippings, hair, whatever. Unless it is told to you, *and you accept it,* it cannot affect you. It is the same exact principle as watching a medical show and having all the symptoms, or looking in somebody's mouth, being afraid that you are going to catch their trench mouth, and acquiring the symptoms. People get very susceptible or suggestible to things—it is almost a psychosomatic type of hypochondria.

Why does everybody want to listen to what people tell them—do they want to be programmed? It is funny that we do not want to listen to anything good, but the bad we absorb right away and begin to relate to it. If someone says, "You will never walk again," then do not answer, "Okay"!

Tools for Protection

Francine: There is a very strong force that is moving, arising from the Mother Goddess and creating a very spiritual rinsing effect. Most spiritual people have had some kind of really strong attack. Symptoms can include not believing in yourself, having the estimation of yourself eroded, all kinds of strange pains, strange futility feelings, thinking "who cares," that type of thing. If not that, then you may feel confusion and wonder, "What is it all for? Why am I so confused? Why is nothing happening? What do I trust?" That is the attack!

You are not going to see a goblin by your bed. That would be easy—you could take a frying pan and let him have it. It is more insidious than that; you feel off-balance and clumsy. The best weapon you have is righteous anger. You have got to focus anger, because righteous anger pierces the darkness.

Be assured that visualizations can help. You can just white-light and purple-light yourself more. When you are under attack, that light dims very quickly during the day, so keep doing it. Do not just do it once in the morning, but also midday and evening. Purple and gold-light yourself, encase yourself in lead, put mirrors around you that reflect outward. Use a symbol of you standing in the middle of a circle of mirrors that face outward. The mirror is one continuous circle with no hinges. Hinges would let light get through. It reflects outward so that any darkness that comes, faces itself. If good comes, it reflects itself and is happy; it gets better. If evil comes and sees itself, it will deflect back.

Be thankful that you know of shelter you can get into, the bomb shelter, when the nuclear darkness fallout comes. That is what they try to do: They literally try to "nuke" you! Put purple and gold light around yourself. Take your warrior stand, wear your Golden Sword at your side, use Azna to walk in beside you, and—most important—call on symbols. Start using Joan of Arc's armor.

Do we chart this, so there is no avoiding it?

Yes. No way of avoiding it. Use Azna's sword that She gives to you freely. Use the circle of mirrors and the mantle of Joan, or anything that has been a symbol throughout history. Use the Golden Chalice— think of drinking from the Chalice of Knowledge so that your tongue will be set free, and you will be able to speak eloquently. Visualize a cross shining behind you, golden and beautiful, not as a representation of something Jesus was hung upon, but something that reaches to the heavens.

Use the dove because it takes flight with purity and freedom. These are the symbols the Gnostics used—the all-seeing eye, the owl of wisdom, and all the symbols that the American Indians have used for many years, their shaman-totems. They were so much smarter than most in their way of using things that were godlike to them or made by God, which were all-seeing and part of nature. Now you must use not only things of nature, but also your own totems and things that have been handed down. The crucifix, the all-seeing eye of knowledge, the chalice, the sword, and the silver light. Nothing can penetrate these symbols.

But all human beings need some symbol. That is why the crucifix has been so powerful. Do you not have a favorite pair of jeans, or a certain type of movie you go to? If you were to look even further, you would see that these are all symbols of your character. Not everyone needs symbols, but everyone should have something that they bring down with them that has power.

I want to give you as many means for protection as possible, because I want to help the positive energy on your planet increase. If your child is having difficulty—perhaps your daughter is expecting, or your son is having mental or physical problems—then you can give them extra protection. It is not idolatry to put a picture of whomever you are worried about in an encasement of glass or in a secured box. Put white light around it, and make sure that there is some ritual of protection. A very powerful thing to do is to put a purple cloth over their picture. In all the churches, the monstrance or chalice was always covered by a purple cloth. That was to give protection and aid in the sanctification of the hosts that rested therein.

Each person is happy and content on our side to their fullest capacity. It is like, "Yes, you have that and I have this, but I like mine better." It is like the thimble and the bucket. Both are full. The thimble does not know there could be more than what is inside it, because it is as full as it can be. But the bucket is also as full as it can be, yet holds so much more.

In this day and age, since you cannot wear shields and masks and armor against the dark entities, I think you had better use something, such as symbols or affirmations. Affirmations are symbols. You are programming affirmations, and that in itself becomes symbolic.

Raheim: What I would do is put myself in a meditative state and increase my aura. You can do all the things that we have talked about with the mirrors and the lead, but more important, ask that their name be written on a blackboard in your mind. When you know their identity, begin to band *them* with light, lead, and mirrors, which blocks them off.

Francine: Another way to obtain this information is to ask God directly. Do it this way: Lie very quietly in your room. Be very quiet, and ask to go to a higher level of consciousness. Say, "Beloved Father and Mother, please take me to the seventh level." Now ask for a message; here is where God's whole mind resides. Say, "Please cleanse me in Your light and identify the source of negativity attacking me." Because it is very easy when you know who your attacker is. I promise you—I guarantee you—that you will get a name or names of people. Once you do this, visualize them encased in lead. You are not going to hurt them. Then surround that lead with a white light to cleanse them.

Stars

Raheim: Now you know very well that there are seven main chakras of the body, located centrally from your head through your torso. I want you to think of each one of these openings in the body as a star. I want you to use a symbol of a star, which we like because it is rounded and yet sharp. Because of its sharp corners, it can close upon itself and make a complete sphere. It can almost be a living entity. Many doctors have viewed this when examining the throat—they come across, literally, a whirlpool of light in the throat area that they cannot explain. These little whirlpool areas are the psychic openings and power centers of the body.

Each of these openings in the body will emit light. Make sure that it does not receive, but puts out. Visualize this as a bright, shining star along with the light that is luminous around you. These lights should pulsate very much like a star blinks and shines so that it is transmitting your light energy. Now you may wonder if this dispels your energy. No—in fact, it is amazing how the more you visualize a star sending out energy, the more strongly it loops around and comes right back to you. As the loop of light bends and gets larger, it encompasses more people, and their light is added to yours. As it comes back, it sprays you with light. So each time your light goes out to someone, it comes back stronger.

You will find that a chakra star has a tingly feeling; this means that it is heating up. I am not just giving you a symbol to use; rather, when we look at you, we see not only your aura, but the actual star in your chakras. You should direct each energy star to shift that energy anyplace that you need it. Sometimes it will shift to a place that you do not think you need it, but actually you do.

However, you must never, ever think of your chakras as being receivers, ever! Always refer to them as *transmitters*. You want them to transmit light and not absorb anything, because once you start absorbing, as you well know, you become too empathetic and start getting ill. You can get too deeply entrenched in someone else's pain or sorrow.

The true healer, which you must all eventually aspire to be, heals not only themselves, but other people. You can heal yourself this way: Literally make the loop of light encompass all those you love, sprinkling them with the light, and then bring it back to yourself. In this way, it will gather the light of others. Say, "I send this loop of light all around the room, to those I love, those I've left at home, and those at my workplace." Do not feel ill-fated in giving up part of your life to help other people, because this is the only way for the true Gnostic.

If you intend to go on with holistic healing arts, this method is really for you. You should do more with it than heal only yourself, because a gift given must also be a gift given away. You cannot keep this knowledge; you must transmit it. The knowledge of Novus Spiritus is meant to be transmitted, not kept secret. Too many organizations insist on hiding their knowledge. Truth is meant to be given to humanity.

Is there any sensation while healing?

Oh, yes, your hands will get warm. Even if you have no sensation at all, healing still comes. It is as if you are a tube and sometimes the water does not hit the sides, but it is certainly running free. It is still working, because you are manifesting and transmitting your energy; you are replacing their energy with yours, and adding your energy to their energy. You can use this for mental, physical, or spiritual healing.

Can we use green candles for healing?

Yes. Anything that has to do with illness of the body is best treated by a green light, especially emerald. But even during your Christmastime, do not light red candles. That always makes me just freeze! Red candles have been used for negative rituals, as have black candles. Everyone wants to use poinsettias and red candles, but they bring in nothing but negative energy. Poinsettia is not a good flower. It has always been a symbol of the blood of Jesus; it carries with it a legend of negativity.

Columns of Light

Raheim: Borrow the strength of what we call columns of light. These huge silver columns that exude a platinum light can be planted anywhere, perhaps right over someone's body. You know the color of platinum; it is deeper than silver. So plant the platinum column with its silvery hue wherever you go. Make this your secret pastime; do it constantly! And whenever you go somewhere, place these columns of light all around—in buildings, in your home, near people you love, and near negative people. With negative people, put it right down on top of them.

This instantly neutralizes negativity. You ask for these beautiful light columns directly from God; you borrow them like Zeus. His lightning bolts were very much like the columns of light; they did not get it totally right, but they certainly knew that God had the power to send light. What you are doing is planting these columns of light so that no one can uproot them. You see, we cannot plant them—you must, in your physical world.

Francine: Columns of light are silvery and iridescent. They give power, in addition to neutralizing evil. When you do it enough, you can almost hear them hum! They literally vibrate. Plant light columns on dark entities. Then run, because this makes them mad! That is not unlike throwing water on the Wicked Witch, from your movie *The Wizard of Oz*. You can almost see them melting.

Every single one of you who plants them helps the world. Each time they are planted, they become stronger. In other words, you will be able to see, feel, and sense them. I know of some people who planted them so strongly that they would literally run into them. That is how strong they became. They would plant them in their house, and in the dark they would run smack into something that seemed to be there, but was really a light column. So do not plant it in a hallway! Put it in a corner over by a plant so you will not be running into it.

What about the sound of bells or running water?

The sound of brass is a wonderful sound. The sound of silver on silver is also wonderful. The sound that will reverberate in your soul is "Om." That is probably one of the most powerful chants you can use, because that is the Sanskrit word for "God." Speak "Om" so that it resonates all the way through your skull.

Bells and running water are wonderful. Tibetan bells, chimes, or brass is marvelous. Glass or ceramic bells do not do much; they just clatter. But anything that has to do with metal is much better. It aligns your chakras to resound. A man by the name of Paul Horne did that inside the Great Pyramid, which is wonderful, or flute music inside the Taj Majal—beautiful sounds.

Can we plant light columns far away?

Oh, yes, you can. You could plant them in Siberia. Start with your own domain first. Make those solid. It is like you do not want to go out and seed somebody else's place until you have been seeded enough yourself. It only takes a few minutes. The more you can visualize, the better—they are not round or square, but triangular in cross-section. It is a three-sided pyramid all the way up. Now I know some of you already saw it like that, but I thought I would tell you.

A Healing Circle Meditation

Raheim: I want you to mentally put a circle in the middle of the room. I want you to reaffirm the power of almighty God, the true Jesus who walks with us, the love of Mother God who surrounds us, and the power of Father God who is our Creator. A beautiful white sparkling shimmer of light begins to form in the circle. Around that circle forms a purple sheath of light as a curtain. It is almost as if the circle now, shimmering as it is, turns into water. The water seems to take on the shades of blue and green. I want you to mentally see a golden light shining directly down from Father God into the center of the circle. Close your eyes now.

Take a deep breath, and put the names of your loved ones in the light, to heal them through God's power. Mentally put in your own name if you so choose. Take a deep breath, and begin to put these people's names into this shimmering, beautiful, emerald green light— the healing waters. A ladle will be dipped out by Azna's hand and administered to them wherever they are, here with us or separate from us. Reaffirm to God Almighty now that you are well and strong.

Say, "I am well. I am strong. I am spiritual. I am blessed. I possess the God-Centeredness. I possess the love and strength of God Almighty. I am on a mission in life to redeem myself and others spiritually. I ask this in God's name. Amen."

Feel the power of God coursing through every cell in your body. Every part of your being that has been darkened or left unattended is now surging with the light and brightness of God.

I leave you with blessings. I leave you with protection. I leave you with the knowledge that if you ever wish to call on me, I am but one tiny thought away.

Crown Chakra Meditation

This is an extensive and powerful healing meditation that can also be used for remote healing. As with everything, the more you use it, the more powerful it becomes.

Usually, when you do a prayer or meditation, you put your hands upward to receive grace. However, for this, put your hands downward on your thighs so nothing escapes from you. Become a funnel; think of a hole appearing at the top of your head that opens right at the crown. Your energy is now self-contained, because you are now becoming a conductor. You are not releasing energy; you are nothing more than a tube of conducted power from God. Coming from God, it begins to flow right through the very top of your head, through the cranial area, moving all the way down through the body like golden water. I want you to feel it like warm water—bathe all your organs in the golden light.

If any part of your body seems ill, let the golden light stop there, whether it is the head, throat, chest area, stomach, or your limbs. Now, when this vibrational current begins to build higher, you will feel that your body begins to warm, to heighten in temperature. At this point, you can then move your own hands, which have been in a downward position, to any part of the body that is affected.

When you do this, I want you to feel that the energy is beginning to pulsate from the top of your head, moving down in a cylindrical form rotating around and bathing out any infected areas of the body that need to be helped. Do not treat more than one area at a time. Each time you do this, you can pick a new area, but you want to give the "full shot" to each area.

Feel your body heating up, and demand that you begin to feel your own pulse. Begin to be aware of the heart beating and pumping strongly. As the heart beats strongly just for a few minutes, the blood elevates—this is not blood *pressure*—the blood begins to course rapidly through the body. If you want to clean something very well, you raise the water line and give much more water, the same as blood. Say, "I want the blood to rise and cleanse, especially the arteries." Make sure you specify that there are no constrictions in the capillaries or arteries. Wherever fresh blood supply can get to, that place is healed.

Now, relax your hands and position them downward on your thighs again. I want you to now transport yourself to an amazingly huge gold pyramid. For a few moments, you are standing outside the pyramid; the next second, you are inside it. Now you can look up through the tiny hole at the apex. Position yourself right in the sunbeam shining through this hole, which is very much like the one I constructed for myself on the Other Side. You do not necessarily look at it, but stand so that you feel the warmth and heat of the sun right where your crown chakra opens.

You now feel a vibratory, God-given energy, which has been known throughout the centuries and is as old as time. It is your own kinetic energy that is now melded and blended with God who imbues and endows you with spirit. As you feel the warmth penetrating, you will now feel all pains, aches, hurts, losses, and disappointments being shed. You will feel them jump from you like shadows. Things long forgotten, things long buried, past-life regrets, karmic experiences that you do not choose to hang on to anymore—all these leap from you. A literal exorcism of your own negative demons of worries!

Feel the heat penetrating you; it is warm, vibratory, stimulating, euphoric, joyous, releasing, free, nonstressful, loving, and giving; it imparts loyalty, honor, steadfastness, and survival! Feel joy invading where despair had been. Two emotions cannot occupy the same place. If there is joy, there cannot be sorrow. If there is health, there cannot be illness. Which do you choose? Choose now, and as they say, "forever after, hold your peace." In your peace, bring it into you in your solar plexus and release everything else. Bring about the soul comfort of harmony. Be very quiet and still. Let God's energy have a chance to fill your destiny with wellness, wholeness, and joyfulness.

Now, bring yourself outside the pyramid. Remember what I have taught you, and bring yourself back to yourself.

Novena for Assistance from Mother Azna

To call on Azna, say: "Azna is our Queen, the Giver of Life, the Great Interceptor, the Miracle Worker, the Fighter of Darkness, the Curer of All Illness." Visualize that *She* stands in front of you with Her beautiful Golden Sword, taking the brunt of this negative energy. Say, "I want this now, *Azna. Please tend to me. Help me now!*"

At 9 A.M. and 9 P.M. daily, say, "I am God. I am part of God. I am God. All things are possible because I am God!" Repeat this three times for three sets: First for yourself, second for others, then a third set for the Gnostic movement of truth!

In addition, the following prayer is very powerful. Say to yourself often, "I am a child of God. I am free of any darkness. I want to be liberated from any force of darkness. I have now accepted the God-Centeredness and the power of Azna, the Mother God, into my heart. My very being is now illuminated in all areas."

The 91st Psalm is probably the most powerful prayer you can use to dispel darkness so that you do not fear the arrows that fly by night.

Use the sacred eye of God. Both the eye and the pyramid are very powerful symbols, of which you can make drawings. Then add the symbol for infinity, which is an eight drawn sideways. Draw it above the pyramid, which represents eternity, and you have three of the most powerful symbols—the infinity of God, the watchful eye of God, and the continual reaching for higher spirituality.

What is the "Guardianship of the Mind"?

When you are addressing both Mother Azna and God the Father, you really should address it also as the "Guardianship of the Mind." This is the direct line to God. It is sort of like trying to call a long-distance number without having the last two digits. Address either the Guardianship of the Mind or the Power Source.

In any situation, ask for and visualize these lights:

- White light—for the Holy Spirit (light white candles)
- Gold light—for your God-Center
- Purple light—for spirituality
- Silver light—calls Azna for emergencies
- Columns of platinum light—for protection
- Green light—for healing and prosperity
- Silver-blue light—for protection from negativity

Take a warrior stand. Use the following:

- Golden sword of Azna—cuts through negativity
- Golden shield of Om—deflects negativity when held in front of you
- Golden hand of Om—the Unmoved Mover holds you
- Golden cross shining behind you—reaches the heavens; a symbol of God-Centeredness

Call on and use the Archangels:

- Michael—Warrior for truth
- Orion—Peacemaker
- Ariel—Message-bringer
- Raphael—Protector
- Gabriel—Healer

Additionally, when you are being attacked, become your totem! Your totem is your own spirit animal. You can also use the devas or energy forces of all inanimate objects. Lilith, Queen of the Fairies, protects children and animals. She closes the door on nightmares.

The following are also positive things to do:

- *Do not withdraw* or isolate yourself from others. Pray, meditate, come to church, and be with other light entities.
- *Use laughter and humor* to dispel negativity.
- *Use righteous anger* to protect your God-Center and temple.
- *Shut windows of negativity* from other people.
- *Cement your aura* around you and expand it outwards; demand that your aura band with white, gold, and purple.
- *Cement your intellect and emotions* together.
- *Follow* a healthy nutritional regime.
- *Cleanse and align your chakras* every day.
- *Wear crystals* to absorb negativity, silver to reflect negativity, or gold to center the self.

Affirmations:

- I want my energy to be boosted and all darkness removed.
- I am a child of God.
- I am free of any darkness.
- I want to be liberated from any dark force.
- I have accepted the God-Centeredness and the power of Azna, the Mother God, into my heart.
- My very being is illuminated in all areas.

- I am empowered with the will of almighty God to be well, to be fruitful, and to be optimistic.
- I am resting in your hands, in your heart, O Mother and Father God.
- Please lead me, direct me, give me peace, and show me the way!

Some symptoms of psychic attack that you may experience are:

- Despair; a feeling of total futility
- Depression
- Anxieties; being riddled with worries not akin to you
- Not believing in yourself; having low self-esteem
- Tiredness and malaise; unease at night; strange dreams; waking up with dread in the morning
- A half-feeling that something is wrong
- A "clawing of the mind"
- Feeling irritable, moody, short-tempered
- Feeling confused, off-balance, and clumsy; feeling that "no one cares"
- Strange physical pains such as nausea, stomachaches in the solar plexus, headaches, backaches, neckaches

჻ ჻ ჻

Prayer for Grace

Dear Father and Mother God,

Let your infusion and grace encompass me and my loved ones.
Let it last throughout all our lives until we are joined with You and
with each other on the Other Side.

Let us not feel alone or sick. We ask for the Holy Spirit's healing grace
to enter every cell of this vehicle we call the body.

Let us link our souls like a giant shaft of light that will appear
for everyone in need.

჻ ჻ ჻ ჻ ჻ ჻

§ Chapter 15 §

Theory of Mind

Sylvia: In 1973, I worked with doctors and psychiatrists at Stanford and Agnew State Hospital, where they were testing all types of paranormal ability. I was also tested by several doctors. Everybody asked me, "How are you doing what you are doing?" So I sat down and tried to put it on paper, as best I could. What came out of that was a very marvelous theory that has helped many people. In fact, many of these doctors are using my theory to balance the mind.

When we come into life, our mind looks like the diagram in Figure 1; the levels go upward from the most basic functions to the most abstract, for most of us. We do not realize that we are cut off at point X, where the superconscious begins. We know that there is a conscious mind, and we have been *told* there is a subconscious mind. I do not buy any of that! We have a conscious and a superconscious mind, as Jung said. If Jung had lived longer, he would have made a great breakthrough.

FIGURE 1: MAP OF THE TRADITIONAL MIND

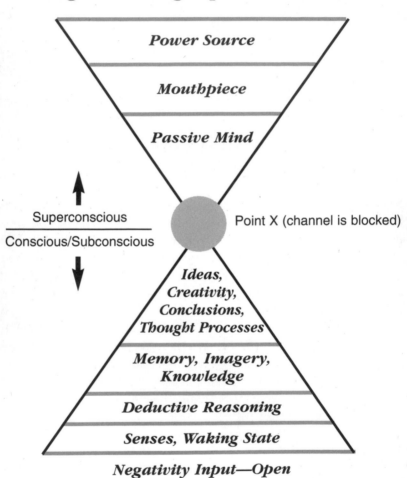

Higher Knowledge Input—The Godhead

Power Source

Mouthpiece

Passive Mind

Superconscious

Conscious/Subconscious

Point X (channel is blocked)

Ideas, Creativity, Conclusions, Thought Processes

Memory, Imagery, Knowledge

Deductive Reasoning

Senses, Waking State

Negativity Input—Open

Intellect dominates left brain, which controls right side of body

Emotion dominates right brai which controls left side of bo

Our Minds

In Figure 1, the two lowest levels are the Senses and Deductive Reasoning, as in: "I see that you have a red sweater on; I know what a sweater is for. That is a tree; it must be one because it looks like other trees I have seen." Moving up, the next level—Memory, Imagery, and Knowledge—stores what the senses have taken in. One cannot possibly store a tree if one does not know what a tree is. The fourth level from the bottom is where we begin to create or draw conclusions based on the three preceding levels. "Now that I have seen a tree and deduced the meaning of a tree, maybe I can draw or do something creative with a tree."

The only problem is that the entire top half—the superconscious—is left out of traditional therapy. It's like not knowing that the highway you're on goes past Podunk. I am telling you the highway can go all the way to the superconscious. Now you have a map and can get there—you can access it from your senses, which are the first level of your conscious mind.

When we come into life, we literally come in with Point X squeezed shut so that we cannot access the superconscious (Figure 1). We all know this is true. What we all have is this big open suction down below the sensing level of the mind, through which we pick up all the garbage of life. It is like having pollution in your brain. We get polluted with noise and other people's thoughts and vibrations, so we cannot discern anymore. We do not know right from wrong.

The first level of the superconscious is the Passive Mind; this is where all your knowledge is stored. This is where your personal Akashic Record is. Isn't that amazingly close? It is not far away, but in your own mind. You have access to it because you are made in the image and likeness of God. The problem is that Point X is so often squeezed shut, so we have no access to the superconscious.

The second level of the superconscious mind, the Mouthpiece, lets us say to God, "I want to be able to speak my knowledge." How many times we have said, "I cannot put it into words. I wish I had said this." When you access this, even in one day, you will become more eloquent. It is like, "I didn't know I could do that." It is as if you are taught something new, like a new hobby, and you go crazy because you know you can finally do it. The third level is the Power Source. This is where you really plug in to God. Every morning when you get up, say, "May the white light of the Holy Spirit surround me, and God, hit it." I mean, the energy, the flood, will come!

FIGURE 2: MAP OF A MIND IN BALANCE

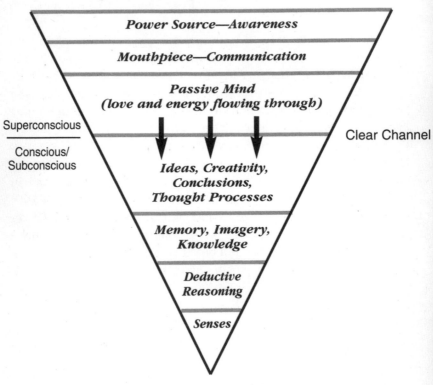

Higher Knowledge Input—The Godhead

Power Source—Awareness

Mouthpiece—Communication

Passive Mind
(love and energy flowing through)

Superconscious

Conscious/
Subconscious

Clear Channel

Ideas, Creativity,
Conclusions,
Thought Processes

Memory, Imagery,
Knowledge

Deductive
Reasoning

Senses

Negativity Shut Out
Intellect and Emotion Balanced

Figure 2 is how we ought to look. I want you to keep this in your mind, how you should look. Notice that Point X has become a clear channel, and the sensory input is squeezed shut. You are no longer a big vacuum cleaner sucking up all kinds of negativity. Keep this second visual in your mind.

See how it looks like a perfect cone? What comes through it is knowledge! It comes right in. You are not squeezed off. You are a perfect upside-down pyramid, a knowledge funnel. You have all your senses, creativity, and deductive and inductive reasoning. You can access the higher power—you can ask for it by name as the Akashic Records, or call it "Passive Mind."

Intellect and Emotion

Keep your mind's intellect and emotion balanced, and do not look at emotion as being the dark side that it was thought to be. Throughout recorded history, those in power have always tried to negate the emotional side of the populace, who were usually women. I am convinced from years of research that psychic ability comes in via the emotional side of the brain. However, the intellect must be there to control it.

People say, "Do not get so emotional. Don't let your emotions run away with you." That is wrong! You are supposed to be emotional— that does not rule out intellect. Intellect is static, like Father God. It is always there, a sentinel figure. But emotion is what creates! You can think about something all day, but unless there is emotion or desire, it will not come about, will it?

All throughout history and in the Bible, women were depicted as bad because they were considered the seat of emotion. This is terrible! It is also connected to scorn for left-handed people, who we now know to be more right-brained. The devil was always supposed to come up on the left. Wrong!

Women have been more prominent as psychics because we are predisposed to be emotional. Let me tell you something. When it resides in a man, not negating us ladies, but they have the best of both worlds. They really do. For one thing, in this terribly prejudiced society, people think men are smarter, do they not? I think when a man is good in terms of psychic ability, he is very good, because men have a more linear mind. But I think it is very hard, because he has got to fight that intellect and override it to get to his emotion. But we women just go with it. We just let it take us, which is fine, because nobody was ever killed by emotion.

What we *are* killed by, however, is letting emotion split us; then we feel insane or out of control. We have all been there, have we not? How many times have we gotten so upset that we say, "I am beside myself!" Or we feel tremendous grief or anger and do not know what to do with ourselves. In these cases, emotion is reigning supreme. But in any healthy mind, intellect will eventually take over. We calm ourselves down: "Oh, wait a minute. I don't want to get irrational." If not, someone will talk to us and reestablish intellectual control.

Now, that is a very important point when discussing the helping professions. A psychic should always be the intellectual control for out-of-whack emotion. This is not to negate psychologists, because they are very important, but psychics can use their emotions, riding along with a person and pulling them back down. We can ride that dark horse with them. Psychics see it in their mind; they are viewing and sensing its vibrations.

In contrast, a psychologist has vast intellectual training yet cannot ride the emotion with their client. They must only go on what is being spoken to them. But the psychic mind says, "Wait a minute, something is off; now I am going to ride along with them to get a sense of it." Then you can ride it as far as they want to go, and then grab them and establish intellectual control until their own intellectual control can take over. But the psychic or therapist does not ever want to keep that intellectual control. If you do, you form groupies, which is so disgusting. Then you get into cults—it's sickening. The good you do in this world should be done for God—who else should know about it?

I don't think there is anything more aggravating than a psychic who tells you about all their hits. When you fully give it up, God is doing it, not you—and that is not to be modest. It is so much better, because the slings and arrows do not hurt you, and the appreciation does not go to your head. Oh, certainly, it affects you on a human level, but you do not get the big head from it, because you know that you are in this world to help other people. It does not carry with it a higher rank than anybody else, trust me—no more than a nurse, doctor, Indian chief, or whatever. You are going to be there to help people; that is the main thing.

So keep your own intellect and emotion in balance. It is marvelous to say every morning, "I want my intellect and emotion to be in balance and cemented together." When you are talking to someone, mentally ask for their intellect and emotion to be cemented together, and for them to be a channel, an energy flow for God's direction. Sometimes, by just establishing intellectual and emotional control for a person, you have done a great service. People will walk out of your room and say, "I'm not sure what they said, but I do feel better." That's the bottom line!

So every morning, think of yourself as a tube, a channel. Set your alarm clock 15 minutes earlier. Don't tell me you need to sleep that extra 15 minutes. What you are going to do with this time is so much better than anything that you could be doing asleep. Line yourself up in the morning—put your intellect and emotion in balance, and ask for the inverted pyramid (Figure 2). Ask for access to the Passive Mind, and to be able to speak your knowledge through the Mouthpiece, and to have the Power Source guide and direct your life. Then surround yourself with the white light of the Holy Spirit. Surround everyone who comes into your life with the white light— whether they like it or not, do it anyway!

ॐ ॐ ॐ

"My soul does magnify the Lord,
and my joy is being because of Him."

— Sylvia

ॐ ॐ ॐ ॐ ॐ ॐ

The Tenets of Novus Spiritus

I

*The way of all peace is to scale the mountain of self.
Loving others makes the climb down easier. We see
all things darkly until love lights the lamp of the soul.*

II

Whatever thou lovest, lovest thou.

III

*Do not give unto God any human pettiness such as
vengeance, wrath, or hate. Negativity is man's alone.*

IV

*Create your own heaven, not a hell.
You are a creator made from God.*

V

*Turn thy power outward, not inward,
for therein shines the Light and the Way.*

VI

*In faith be like the wind chimes, hold steady until faith,
like the wind, moves you to joy.*

VII

*Know that each life is a path winding toward
perfection. It is the step after step that is hard,
not the whole of the journey.*

VIII

*Be simple. Allow no man to judge you,
or even yourself, for you cannot judge God.*

IX

*You are a light in a lonely,
dark desert that enlightens many.*

X

*Let no one convince you that you are less than a God.
Do not let fear imprison your spiritual growth.*

XI

*Do not allow the unfounded belief in demons to
block your communion with God.*

XII

*The body is a living temple unto God,
wherein we worship the spark of the Divine.*

XIII

*God does not create the adversities in life.
By your own choice they exist to aid in your perfection.*

XIV

*Karma is nothing more than honing the wheel
of evolvement. It is not retribution, but
merely a balancing of experiences.*

XV

*God allows each person the opportunity for perfection,
whether you need one life or a hundred lives to reach
your level of perfection.*

XVI

*Devote your life, your soul, your very existence
to the service of God. For only there will you
find meaning in life.*

XVII

War is profane, defense is compulsory.

XVIII

*Death is the act of returning Home; it should be
done with grace and dignity. You may preserve that
dignity by refusing prolonged use of artificial life
support systems. Let God's will be done.*

§ § § € € €

ॐ About the Author ॐ

Millions of people have witnessed **Sylvia Browne's** incredible psychic powers on TV shows such as **Montel Williams, Larry King Live,** and **Unsolved Mysteries;** she has also been profiled in **Cosmopolitan, People** magazine, and other national media. Her on-target psychic readings have helped police solve crimes, and she astounds audiences wherever she appears. Sylvia is the author of **Adventures of a Psychic, Life on the Other Side,** and **The Other Side and Back,** among other works.

ॐ ॐ ॐ

Contact Sylvia Browne at:
www.sylvia.org
or
Sylvia Browne Corporation
35 Dillon Ave.
Campbell, CA 95008
(408) 379-7070

Other Hay House Titles of Related Interest

BOOKS

Born to Be Together: *Love Relationships, Astrology, and the Soul,*
by Terry Lamb

Colors & Numbers:
Your Personal Guide to Positive Vibrations in Daily Life,
by Louise L. Hay

The Experience of God:
How 40 Well-Known Seekers Encounter the Sacred,
edited by Jonathan Robinson

Experiencing the Soul:
Before Birth, During Life, After Death,
by Eliot Jay Rosen

Infinite Self:
33 Steps to Reclaiming Your Inner Power,
by Stuart Wilde

The Lightworker's Way:
Awakening Your Spiritual Power to Know and Heal
by Doreen Virtue, Ph.D.

Magi Astrology™:
The Key to Success in Love and Money
by The Magi Society®

AUDIOS

Psychic and Intuitive Healing,
by Barbara Brennan, Rosalyn Bruyere, and Judith Orloff, M.D.,
with Michael Toms

Tools for Success:
Learning to Change Your Thoughts and Change Your Life,
by Louise L. Hay

The Ways of the Mystic:
7 Paths to God
by Joan Borysenko, Ph.D.
(also available as a book under the title *7 Paths to God)*

Notes

Notes

Notes

Notes

Notes

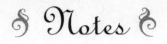

Notes

Notes